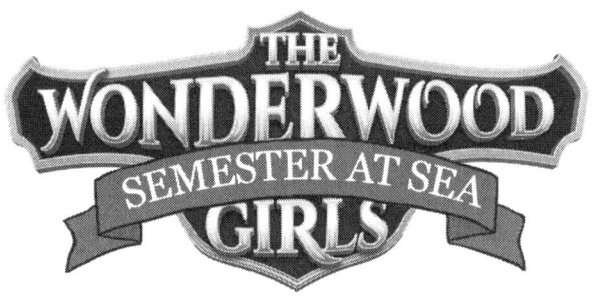

Curt Wilkinson

blueparkbooks
www.blueparkbooks.com

Copyright ©2024 by Curt Wilkinson

Published by BLUE PARK BOOKS, LLC

All rights reserved. For information about permission to reproduce selections from this book, write to Permissions, Blue Park Books, 123 Roark Hls, Branson, MO 65616

Publisher's Cataloging-in-Publication P-CIP Data

Wilkinson, Curt (Curtis A.)

    The Wonderwood Girls / Curt Wilkinson
    p. cm.

Summary: Ten girls and their professors have been forced to leave their campus and pursue the semester at sea. The girls arrive in the Galápagos Islands only to find more trouble waiting and the challenge of a lifetime.

The story, names, characters, and incidents in this book are all fictitious. No identification with actual persons (living or deceased), is intended or should be inferred.

ISBN: 978-1-7337250-6-4

Library of Congress Control Number: 2023924663

1. Adventure   2. Chapter Book   3. Middle Grade
4. Books for Girls   5. Fiction

I. Title:	The Wonderwood Girls
II. Title:	Semester at Sea
III. Title:	Book Two

Fiction │ Paperback

Printed in the United States of America

For Deb

Thanks for your honest critiques and enduring encouragement.
16 68 15 72 55 18 02 19 80 28 40 30 77

For more
information on the series:

wonderwoodgirls.com

Meditare Miraculum

PURSUE WONDER

Wonderwood Academy

Founded 1961

CONTENTS

MAPS

FLIGHT TO ECUADOR
Page 13

THE GALÁPAGOS ISLANDS
Page 14

BEAGLE BAY MAPS
Page 15

CHAPTERS

01 The Airport 17

02 The Galápagos 27

03 The SS Seadoodle 37

04 Hector the Inspector 45

05 The Earth Protectors 57

06 Life at Sea 65

07 Sausage and Ciphers 75

08 The Southern Cross 83

09 Aquadoodles 91

10 Seaweed Rescue 99

11 I've Got Your Back 107

12 Facing the Consequences 115

13 Poison in Your Pocket 123

CHAPTERS (Continued)

14 Radio Waves..129

15 Hector's Ultimatum....................................137

16 Ruth's Fan Cam..145

17 The Pelican...155

18 The Secret Meeting....................................161

19 Midnight Mission......................................169

20 On the Island...175

21 The Longest Night.....................................183

22 Colossus Speaks.......................................191

23 Faith is All You Need.................................199

24 The Escape..205

25 The SS Toothache......................................213

26 Sinking Down..221

27 Lily Goes to the Dentist.............................225

28 The Black Wolf..233

29 The Countdown...239

30 Bombs Away..243

31 Chaos in the Bay......................................247

32 All Washed Up...253

MAPS

FLIGHT TO ECUADOR

CHICAGO

THE WONDERWOOD GIRLS ACADEMY

MIAMI

THE GALÁPAGOS ISLANDS

QUITO
ECUADOR

600 MILES

GALÁPAGOS ISLANDS

PINTA

GENOVESA

MARCHENA

SANTIAGO   **Beagle Bay**
See map on next page.

FERNANDINA   BALTRA

SANTA CRUZ

SANTA FÉ

SAN CRISTÓBAL

ISABELA

FLOREANA   ESPAÑOLA

80 MILES

BEAGLE BAY

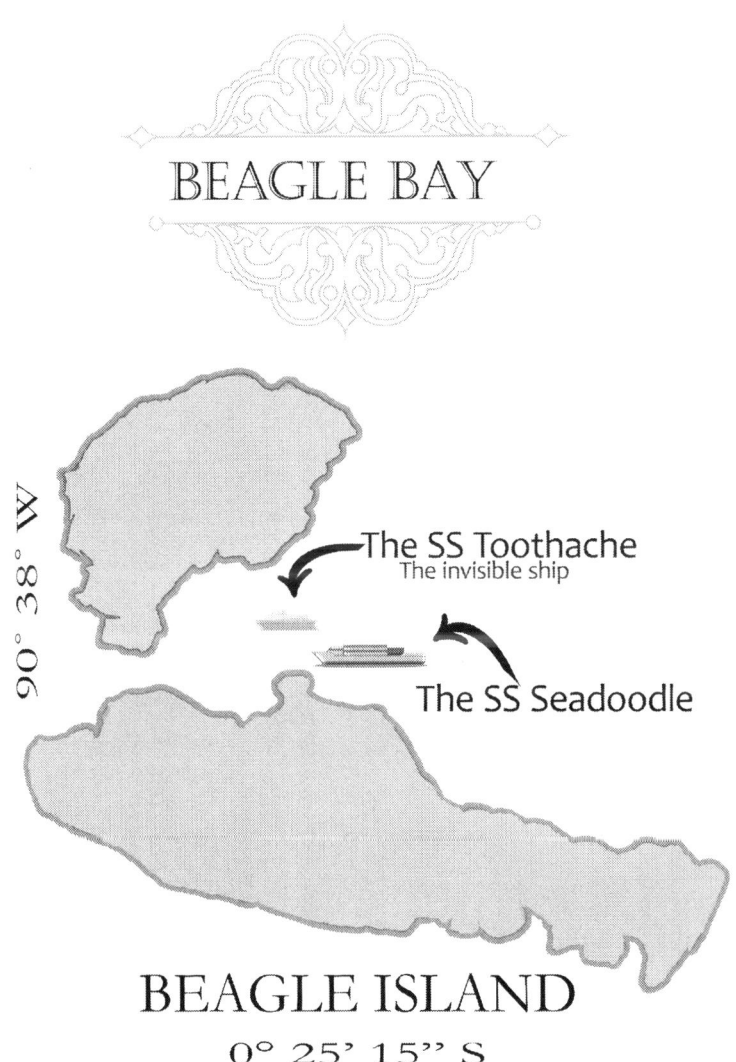

90° 38' W

The SS Toothache
The invisible ship

The SS Seadoodle

BEAGLE ISLAND
0° 25' 15'' S

1
THE AIRPORT

NOTE: It is important to mention that this chapter takes place only a few hours after the disastrous events of book one, which are now forcing the Wonderwood Academy to leave the country.

The Wonderwood Girls arrived at the Chicago airport looking like a worn-out band of rejects from a traveling dog show. Ten dogs, ten girls, and their twelve professors stumbled out of a bus and onto the sidewalk just outside the terminal. A cargo truck pulled up behind them, and two men started unloading bags, boxes, and dog cages of assorted sizes. Four men from airport security rushed out to get things under control.

"Hey, get these dogs out of here!" shouted the head officer. "This isn't a circus. Now clear the sidewalk!"

"We're sorry," said Dr. Tusen-Takk, "but we do have permission from the president."

"Yeah right, lady, and I'm the king of Sweden," said the officer.

"Please, sir, I'm not joking," said Dr. Tusen-Takk as she handed him a document with the official seal of the U.S. government.

"Oh, so you're the group from the Wonderwood Academy! They told us to be expecting you. I didn't think you'd have so many dogs!"

The security officer immediately ordered his team to assist the girls into the terminal, and then he grabbed his radio to request additional support.

"Where are you headed?" asked the officer.

"Ecuador, South America," said Dr. Tusen-Takk. "The Galápagos Islands to be exact. We've been forced to conduct this semester at sea."

"Forced?" said the officer.

"Yes, I'm afraid our campus was destroyed by terrorists."

"Terrorists?"

Dr. Tusen-Takk raised her hand to cover her lips. Did she just say terrorists? She couldn't believe it was true, but it was. The Russian mega-corporation Colossus had been officially recognized as a terrorist organization just a few hours earlier that day. It was discovered they had plans to take over strategic points of power all over the world.

"I'm sorry officer, but I've already said too much," Dr. Tusen-Takk apologized. "Now, if you'll please excuse us, we have a plane to catch."

A small army of airline attendants, baggage boys, and airport representatives descended on the Wonderwood team and began to gather their things.

"My dog has been injured," said Lily to the woman who was assisting her.

"I can see that. Did he fall?"

"No, a bomb exploded and broke his leg," replied Lily without thinking.

"A bomb?" said the woman. "That's not a word you want to hear at an airport."

"It's a word you don't want to hear anywhere!" said Lily.

"Well, let's get him in a wheelchair, and I'll roll him to the security gate."

"His name is Cousteau," said Lily, "and he's a hero!"

"They're both heroes," said Lady Burd, putting her hand on Lily's shoulder. "Half our team wouldn't be here if it weren't for these two."

Lily blushed in embarrassment.

"It's a great story, but we'll have to save it for another time," said Lady Burd. "Let's hurry along now. We need to pass through security. I can tell you from years of passing through security checkpoints all over the world, this isn't going to be easy!"

Lady Burd was right. Dr. Tusen-Takk immediately made a phone call to the Ecuadorian Embassy in Washington, DC. It turns out it was not the students and professors that were difficult to pass through customs; it was the Wonder Doodles!

"Beth, are all our dogs up to date with their shots and health certificates?" asked Dr. Tusen-Takk.

"Yes, everything is in order," said Beth confidently. "We

just need the Ecuadorian consulate to approve it, but that usually takes a couple months!"

"I'm on the phone with the Ecuadorian ambassador as we speak," said Dr. Tusen-Takk. "Let's assume we'll be approved here shortly. Start getting the Wonder Doodles in their cages and ready to pass through security."

The Wonderwood team spent the next two hours checking their bags, answering questions, and passing through security scanners. When they finally arrived at their departure gate, Lady Burd gathered the group for some brief instructions.

"Everyone, listen up!" Lady Burd shouted. "I want to give you a rundown of what our schedule looks like for the next twelve hours. We're about to fly to the Galápagos Islands in Ecuador, South America. We're on what's called a 'The Red Eye' flight. That means we'll be flying all night, with a brief stop in Miami and a short layover in the capital city of Quito. The good news is we don't have to get off the plane during layovers, we've been cleared to stay on the plane until we reach our destination. We'll arrive in Galápagos early tomorrow morning, so I suggest you try getting some sleep on the plane, you're going to need lots of energy. Tomorrow, we hit the ground running!'"

Evie raised her hand. "Lady Burd, I saw a bookstore in the airport, and I was wondering if I could look for a book about Ecuador and the Galápagos Islands. I also want to get some snacks for the plane."

Lady Burd looked at Evie with concern.

"Evie, I don't want to seem overly cautious or afraid, but I know the people who destroyed our school will stop at nothing to shut the academy down. So, on this trip, these are the rules: If you want to leave the group and explore, you must never go alone. You've all been assigned a roommate, so make sure you stick together. Whenever we leave to travel from one place to another, I'll call for a team check. I want you to look at each other and say, 'I've got your back!'"

"Great!" said Evie as she gave Natasha a huge bear hug. "Nati, I've got your back!"

Evie released her roommate and turned to give Lady Burd a rib-crushing hug. "Lady Burd, I've got your back too!"

Lady Burd laughed, "Okay girls, you can go," she said looking at the group, "but stay together, and remember to be back here forty-five minutes before our flight is scheduled to depart!"

Isabela Cruz looked over at Lily Fernbush. "Do you and Abby-Marie want to get some snacks for the flight? Faith and I are going have a look around the airport."

"Abby-Marie?" said Faith, looking around the terminal. "Where is she?"

"I don't know," said Lily. "I saw her going through the security scanners, but that was thirty minutes ago."

The three girls looked around the waiting area and spotted Abby-Marie sitting in a row of chairs next to the wall. She was bent over with her head to her knees, and her face was buried in her hands. Abby-Marie was doing her best to hide the tears running down her cheeks.

Lily ran over to check on her friend. "Abby-Marie, what's the matter?"

"Yeah, what's the matter?" Isabela chimed in. "Aren't you excited? We're going to Ecuador! You're going to meet my mom and dad! We're going to the Galápagos Islands!"

"That might be great for you," sobbed Abby-Marie, "but I'm terrified!"

"Terrified?" asked Lily as she sat down next to her roommate. "What do you mean terrified?"

"I looked it up," said Abby-Marie. "I think I have thalassophobia."

"Thalassa what?" said Faith.

"Thalassophobia. It's the fear of the ocean, the sea, and large bodies of water. I hate the water. I don't want anyone to know."

"Wow!" said Lily. "Haven't you ever been to a swimming pool or taken a holiday by the sea? How do you hide something like that?"

"I always say I'd rather sit on the beach and read a book," said Abby-Marie. "Most people never seem to have a problem with that, but I don't think I can avoid it for a whole semester at sea! I'm thinking about calling my mom and dad and asking if I can go home."

Isabela handed Abby-Marie a tissue. "Oh, Abby-Marie, don't be silly! We're not the Wonderwood Girls without you. Besides, I have so many amazing things I want to show you! You're just being a coward!"

Isabela paused as a large man with a massive mustache

walked past the four girls and sat in one of the chairs in front of them.

Abby-Marie looked up at the man, and her heart went cold with fear. "Can we go somewhere else and talk?" she whispered.

The man could tell he made the girls feel uncomfortable. He was an exceptionally large man, with rippling muscles, a bald head. He also had the most massive mustache the girls had ever seen.

"C'mon," said Lily, "Let's join the rest of the group."

The man nervously picked up a cardboard box and placed it on his lap trying to protect the contents inside.

Isabela leaned in close to her friends and whispered intensely. "Do you see that?"

The girls looked at the large box the man cradled in his hands. The box was branded with a logo they had all seen before. Large black letters formed the word COLOSSUS.

"They're here!" whispered Lily. "It's Colossus. They're following us!"

2
THE GALÁPAGOS

"Ladies and gentlemen, we will now begin boarding flight 467 to Miami, with a final destination of Ecuador and the Galápagos Islands. Please have your boarding passes ready."

As people grabbed their bags and hurried to the gate, the man with the Colossus box and the massive mustache stood up and disappeared into the crowd. All the Wonderwood professors and students gathered around Abby-Marie, who was fighting back tears.

"We're not going without you!" said Lily. "You're my roommate!"

"Lily is right," said Lady Burd. "We need to go together. We're a team, and we go together, or we don't go at all. That's what it means to 'have your back.'"

After a long round of pleading and begging, Abby-Marie reluctantly agreed to get on the plane with the rest of the group. Everyone settled into their seats and prepared for a long night on the plane. Several girls purchased those inflatable neck pillows and asked for blankets. Most people were too excited to sleep.

"In the morning we'll all be in Ecuador!" Isabela cheered.

Abby-Marie covered her head with a blanket and plugged her ears. "Oh, calm down!" she whispered to herself. "You're really starting to annoy me."

The sun was just beginning to break the horizon when the Wonderwood team raised the blinds on their windows.

"Ladies and gentlemen, we will be landing in just a few minutes," a flight attendant interrupted. "Please return your tray tables and seat backs to their full, upright position. The local time is 6:57 a.m. and the current temperature is 86 degrees. Welcome to the Galápagos Islands!"

When the plane landed, Lady Burd stood up with instructions. "Everyone, listen up! Dr. Tusen-Takk has informed me that there will be someone from the Ecuadorian government to help us pass through security. Please have your passports ready and be prepared to attend to your dogs."

As the Wonderwood Girls and their professors landed on the island of Baltra, everyone immediately felt like they were in a mystical, magical place.

"It feels like we've landed on another planet!" said Ruth.

"Well, this is the closest thing to it," replied marine biologist Dr. Maribel Martinez. "The Galápagos Islands are one of the most unique places on earth. We're standing on lava rocks formed by volcanoes! It may seem like a rugged place, but it's also fragile and the plants and wildlife need to be protected. That's one of the reasons we're here!"

As the Wonderwood Girls passed through security and customs, they were led to the baggage claim expecting to hear the sound of ten barking puppies. Instead, there was silence.

"Where are the Wonder Doodles?" asked Grace. "The plane is empty; all our luggage is here. Where is Einstein?"

"Your dogs were detained," said a man in uniform standing directly behind them. "I'm afraid I have some bad news, but first, please allow me to introduce myself. My name is Hector Muñoz, and I am the inspector of wildlife conservation here on the Galápagos Islands. As you know, these islands are a protected marine reserve. I represent the Ecuadorian government, and we cannot risk the possibility of your dogs bringing contagious diseases to the wildlife we have been charged to protect."

"But we have special clearance!" insisted Professor Broomfield. "We spoke with your highest officials at the Ecuadorian embassy!"

"Perhaps," responded Director Muñoz, "but no one has spoken to me, and without my authority, no pets of any kind are allowed on these islands!"

"So where are they?" questioned Dr. Tusen-Takk. "One of those dogs is injured, he has a broken leg!"

"Your dogs are just fine," said Director Muñoz. "They're being kept in quarantine. We need to be sure they are not caring any infectious diseases."

"But…," pleaded Dr. Tusen-Takk.

"No but," ordered Director Muñoz. "I must protect the

islands!" He snapped to attention and offered a formal military salute. "Enjoy your time here in the Galápagos!"

Dr. Tusen-Takk quickly looked at Dr. Broomfield and Dr. Thomsen, who were responsible for the doodles' medical papers. "Ladies let's start making some phone calls. I thought we had this covered! We need the doodles to be with us this semester. Without them, well… We wouldn't be the Wonderwood Academy!"

The two professors grabbed their phones and ran after the inspector.

"Now what do we do?" asked Mikako.

"We get to our ship," responded Lady Burd confidently. "Grab your things. We're expected to board in less than an hour."

The girls quickly grabbed their luggage and boarded the shuttle bus that was waiting for them outside.

"Everyone accounted for and ready to go?" asked Lady Burd once the girls were seated. "Do we have each other's backs?"

"Not really," said Evie Kron as she pointed out the window.

Abby-Marie was standing motionless on the sidewalk trying not to scream. She held her backpack in front of her for protection.

"Help! It's a dragon. I think he's going to eat me!" she screamed, trying not to anger the large reptile standing in front of her.

"It's not a dragon!" shouted Isabela, "It's an iguana!" She rushed out of the bus to rescue Abby-Marie. "Don't worry, they don't eat little girls from France! They only like to eat little girls from England!"

"Not funny," said Lily as Isabela and Abby-Marie returned to the shuttle bus and plopped in their seats.

Lily rushed over to sit next to Abby-Marie. "How are you holding up?" she asked whispering so no one could hear. "Are you ready to get on that boat?"

"We'll see," answered Abby-Marie. "I'm beginning to think the bigger question is if I'm ready to get on that boat with Isabela Cruz. She can be so annoying!"

The group sat quietly in the bus as they drove to their new floating campus. It was almost too much to take in. The girls had very little sleep the night before, their dogs were gone, and now they were looking out the window at a strange island preparing to spend the semester at sea.

"It's dock number 17," Lady Burd said to the driver. "We're looking for a ship named Seadoodle."

The bus pulled up to a large research vessel tied to the dock. The name Seadoodle had been freshly painted on the forward bow. Isabela's parents waved from the deck above. On the dock below, there were crates and boxes stacked high and filled with supplies for the semester ahead.

"Hurry!" cried Isabela. "I want to see my mom and dad!"

As the girls pulled their luggage from the compartments below the bus, a taxi pulled up on the opposite side. The man with the massive mustache stepped out and pulled a small slip of paper from his pocket, checking to see if he was in the right location. As he stepped forward, Abby-Marie looked under the bus to the opposite side and recognized the man's big black boots.

"Lily, it's him!" she whispered intensely.

"Who?" asked Lily.

"The man with the massive mustache! The man with the Colossus box!"

Lily looked around and motioned for the girls to come together in a huddle. "Ruth," she said in panic, "What do we do?"

Ruth stared back at Lily trying to figure out what to do next. "Girls, we have to surprise this guy. Everyone, hide behind a crate or box or something. We have to take out Mr. Mustache!"

"What's the signal?" asked Anna.

"I don't know," said Ruth. "Signal?"

"How about a barbaric yawp?" said Anna. "It's from a famous Walt Whitman poem. I've always wanted to try it."

"Okay, great," said Ruth. "We attack when I yawp!"

The girls took their positions and watched as the yellow taxi drove away. The large man put the piece of paper back in his pocket and stooped to pick up his luggage. The girls leaned forward and looked over at Ruth. She raised her hand and screamed.

"YAWP!"

All at once, the girls pounced on the man from behind. Anna gave him a swift kick in the knees while Grace grabbed him around the waist. Four girls latched onto his arms while two more attacked his ankles below. Ruth wrapped her arms around his neck and grabbed his massive mustache from both sides of his head. The man tumbled to the ground with a swarm of Wonderwood Girls piled on top of him.

"Help!!! Inge!" he cried. "It's me! It's me, Sven!"

3

THE SS SEADOODLE

Dr. Tusen-Takk gasped. "Sven? Is that you?" The head chancellor, who was usually prim and proper, was obviously shaken. "Girls, stop! That man is my cousin!"

The girls peeled off one by one as the large man stood and dusted himself off. "Ya, it's me, Sven."

"We're sorry," said Ruth, attempting to return part of the mustache she pulled from his upper lip.

Sven Torgenson stood six feet, eight inches tall. He was an incredibly large Norwegian man with a massive mustache and a shiny bald head. He could have competed in bodybuilding competitions, but that was the furthest thing from his mind. The only thing Sven wanted to do was cook.

"Wow, you've lost a lot of hair!" smiled Dr. Tusen-Takk, stepping up to give her cousin a hug. "I barely recognized you."

"Well, you haven't changed a bit," smiled Sven in return, "except for that bump on your forehead."

"*Uf-dah!*" sighed Dr. Tusen-Takk, reaching up to feel the swollen bump. "It's a long story," she replied, "but right now, I'm more curious to know what you're doing here. I thought you were working in Alaska!"

"I was, but that job ended. I was heading back to Norway when I received an urgent job posting for a head chef position on a small research ship in the Galápagos Islands. Is this the Seadoodle?" he asked, pointing to the ship docked in front of them.

"Girls!" Dr. Tusen-Takk turned around to face the group with delight. "This is my cousin Sven Torgenson, and he will be joining us this semester as our head chef!"

"Hurray!" everyone cheered, everyone except for Lily. She snarled under her breath and kicked the box on the ground next to Sven's feet.

"Colossus!" she whispered. "I hate Colossus."

Isabela couldn't contain herself any longer. "Can we go aboard now? I want to see my mom and dad!"

"Of course," replied Dr. Tusen-Takk. "I'm sorry to have made you wait. Why don't you run ahead? We'll catch up and bring your things."

Isabela took off, losing a flip-flop as she scurried up the ramp to the deck where her mom and dad were waiting to greet her.

Abby-Marie wasn't so eager. She grabbed Lily's hand as a feeling of nausea surged from her stomach.

"You've got this," said Lily.

Abby-Marie grimaced. "Wonderwood Academy?" she thought, "Where's the wonder? Where's the woods?"

"Hurry, everyone, I want you to meet my family! This is my dad, Carlos Cruz; he's the captain. And this is my mom, Nina Cruz; she's a marine biologist and head of research."

"Welcome aboard the Seadoodle!" said Captain Carlos. "We're so glad you're here. We know you're tired from your trip, so let's get your things on board so we can be on our way. Our destination is a quiet little bay with beautiful views. You're going to love it!"

"Where should we put our luggage?" asked Grace.

"Good question," answered Isabela's mom. "I'll show you to your cabins. I'm afraid you didn't give us much time. We've been working from the second we heard you were coming; we've barely had enough time to get supplies and fuel. In fact, I just finished painting the name on the bow of the ship five minutes ago!"

The girls looked over the railing and saw the letters S-E-A-D-O-O-D-L-E.

"We do apologize," responded Dr. Tusen-Takk. "I was thinking we were going to have to cancel the semester altogether. The events of the last week have presented us with some exceedingly difficult circumstances."

"Nothing the Wonderwood Girls can't handle!" replied Lady Burd. "We're up for a challenge, aren't we, girls? Especially after all we've been through together."

"That's right!" Ruth responded, and she let out another exuberant "YAWP!"

Sven covered his mustache to protect himself, "Please, no more yawps!"

"Yes, please girls, no more yawps," responded Lady Burd. "Now who's ready to get settled in and explore this amazing ship?"

Captain Carlos made his way to the bridge to get the Seadoodle underway, as Nina Cruz led the group on a brief tour of the ship. They all gathered on the main deck which was open and spacious providing lots of room for whale-watching and taking in the salty air. On one side was a double door that opened to a large dining hall.

"Looks like we'll be having some great meals together!" said Anna Andersen, looking over at Sven.

"Ya, you bet!" said Sven, "But... if we're going to have anything to eat at all, I need to start cooking right now. Where's the kitchen?"

"It's right here," said Nina as she opened a door that exposed a small kitchen galley. It was designed to feed a small crew of scientists, not ten girls and their twelve professors. Sven could see he had lots of work to do if he was going to get the kitchen ready for the semester. He began wiping down the countertops and rearranging pots and pans.

"*Uf-dah*," said Sven. "Would it be possible to move lunch

back an hour? It's going to take a couple hours to get this kitchen cleaned up!"

"Our biggest challenge is going to be how to set up boarding facilities for the Wonder Doodles," said Nina, as the rest of the group headed down a narrow staircase on the other side of the kitchen. "I'm not so sure this ship was designed to handle ten energetic doodle dogs!"

"That is if they ever get here!" replied Lady Burd. "One of the officials at the airport told us they would be held indefinitely in quarantine!"

"Oh, did you run into my brother Hector the Inspector?" asked Nina. "He's not so tough. Did he give you the old 'I must protect the islands!' line?"

"Do you think you could put in a good word for us?" asked Dr. Tusen-Takk. "Beth and Brigitte have been trying to work things out with the ambassador, but Hector wasn't budging. He's made it very clear that protecting the Galápagos was a global concern!"

"I'll see what I can do," said Nina. "From what Isabel has told me, a semester without the doodles at the Wonderwood Academy is hardly a semester at all."

As the group passed through the long, narrow hallways, they saw large holding tanks containing fish and other sea life. Other rooms were filled with scuba tanks, wetsuits, and crates containing research instruments. It was clear the ship was designed to do scientific research at sea.

"I know this ship is a world-class research vessel," said Dr. Khumalo, "but do you really think we can get it set up for a semester at sea? How are we going to survive with ten girls, ten dogs, and the rest of us?"

"I'm afraid we don't have many alternatives," said Lady Burd. "I say we lean in and make it work."

When the girls found their cabins and dropped off their belongings, Nina led the group back up to the main deck and then up a flight of stairs to the captain's bridge. At the steering wheel, Captain Carlos was setting a course on the navigation system. Carlos had worked hard to make the Seadoodle one of the best marine research vessels in the world. It was a ship filled with the latest technology, and it was obvious he couldn't wait to show it off.

"Girls, I invite you to look out over the bow of the ship to the horizon. Do you see that small island ahead? That's Beagle Island. It's uninhabited and has one of the most beautiful sea coves in all of the Galápagos. We have been using it as our home base for over ten years. If we're lucky, there should be a small pod of dolphins waiting for us when we arrive."

As everyone turned their heads to look for dolphins, Grace Middletree turned her head in the opposite direction. She looked up in the sky behind the ship and saw a flying object chasing the Seadoodle.

"Captain Cruz?" said Grace nervously. "Are we expecting company?"

Isabela's father turned and saw a large military helicopter racing toward them. The helicopter hovered overhead, and a man with a large megaphone leaned out the open cargo door.

"Captain, stop your vessel! That's an order!"

4

HECTOR THE INSPECTOR

"It's Colossus! Quick! Everyone get below deck!" shouted Dr. Tusen-Takk.

The girls immediately ran out the door with their professors and Dr. Tusen-Takk close behind. In her panic, the tall chancellor slammed her head on the opening of the door and fell to the floor.

"Ugh! Not again!" gasped Lady Burd. "Dr. Donsky, would you please look after Dr. Tusen-Takk? I need to get the girls below!"

The voice from the helicopter repeated the command over the megaphone.

"Captain, stop your vessel! That's an order!"

"Hector? Is that you?" Captain Cruz pulled back on the throttle and brought the Seadoodle to a complete stop. He rushed down the stairs and onto the deck below as the helicopter positioned itself directly overhead. The chopper blades produced a powerful blast of air that made it almost impossible to stand.

"What are you doing?" screamed Captain Cruz to his brother-in-law above him. "Are you crazy?"

Hector the Inspector stowed his megaphone and strapped himself into a safety harness connected to a cable and motorized winch. He turned back into the hold of the helicopter and hoisted a fluffy white Dalmadoodle with a broken leg into his arms. The helicopter crew lowered Hector and the puppy down to the deck of the ship.

"Cousteau!" screamed Lily, peering through the porthole from the deck below. "Lady Burd, can I go on deck? Please, oh please!!!"

Lady Burd couldn't even finish saying, "No, it's not saf..." before the small girl from England with big ears and a photographic memory wriggled her way out of the door and onto the main deck. The force of air produced by the helicopter blades immediately flattened Lily to the deck. She looked up and made eye contact with Cousteau. Lily started crawling on all fours, slowly making her way to the man who was holding him.

"Please, sir," she pleaded, "may I have my puppy?"

Cousteau jumped from the inspector's arms and landed on Lily's belly. The two embraced as Cousteau licked her face and neck, ignoring the pain that was shooting through his leg.

"You better get your friends!" shouted the inspector. "There's nine more of these guys we have to deliver." Lady Burd and Mitch Middletree rushed out to help pull Lily and Cousteau to safety.

"Hector, how can we help?" asked Lady Burd.

"Well, we have nine more of these dogs up there, and they all need to get down here. We'll start with the biggest ones and end with the smallest."

They looked over their heads, and a large Saint Berdoodle was being lowered in a basket.

"Who owns the Saint Bernard?"

Lady Burd turned to Mitch. "Mitch, take Lily and

Cousteau to the dining hall. Then get the girls ready to come out and get their doodles. Faith Nkosi is first. Copernicus is on his way down. He wants to send them down largest to smallest, so get the girls lined up and ready to go. The faster we get this helicopter out from over our heads the better!"

Mitch grabbed Lily's hand and helped pull her to her feet. He picked up Cousteau and hurried the girl and her puppy back to cover in the dining hall.

"Stay here!" Mitch said to Lily. "I'm going to bring out the rest of the girls. We'll send them out one by one to get their doodles."

Mitch gave Cousteau a friendly pat on the head. "Good to see you, boy!" he said and then rushed out the door and back onto the main deck.

"Girls, we have a special delivery this morning!" Mitch shouted as he led the group up to the dining hall. "Faith, Anna, and Isabela you're up first. It's Doodle Day all over again!"

Faith Nkosi from South Africa, age eight, was struggling to be brave. She walked out on deck and looked up at the basket over her head.

"It's okay, Copernicus. I've got you!" she said with fake

confidence. Copernicus jumped from the basket and surrounded the little girl with fur as if to say, "You've got me? No, I've got you!" Faith grabbed his collar, and Copernicus dragged her back to safety.

Next was Anna Andersen from Denmark, age twelve, tall and confident. She marched out on deck to collect her Huskydoodle, Gutenburg. She was a little scared too but she did her best not to let it show.

Isabela followed and rushed out to give her uncle Hector a big hug. "¡*Gracias, tío*!" she screamed. "Thanks for bringing me Galileo!" Her doodle was a large Airedoodle, and he didn't seem to be enjoying the delivery process at all.

Next lining up to take their turn were Grace Middletree, age eleven, from the United States; Mikako Fujimora, age eleven, from Japan; and Evie Kron, age ten, from Israel. Grace rushed out and pulled Einstein, her bassetoodle from the basket. Mikako did the same, covering Newton, her Jackapoo, with her jacket to protect him from the wind. Evie felt less confident, as she decided to crawl on the deck to pick up her goldendoodle, Pascal.

Ruth Middletree, age twelve, from Canada, and Natasha Petrov, age nine, from Russia, decided to walk out together. Ruth pulled her border doodle, Joey, from the basket and then waited with her friend as the basket lowered again with Nati's cute little Peekapoo named DaVinci.

"Is that it?" asked Lady Burd.

Hector held up one finger. "There's one more!"

Lady Burd waved to Mitch to send out Abby-Marie Dupree, age ten, from France, but she didn't come. Lady Burd rushed to the dining hall to see what the problem was.

"She's afraid," said Mitch. "She doesn't want to go out on deck. She says she's afraid Edison will wash overboard." Lady Burd looked at Abby-Marie. "Will you go if I go with you? You can even close your eyes. I think you'll regret it if you don't go claim your doodle."

Abby-Marie thought of her furry little Maltipoo, Edison, and how much she missed him.

"Okay," said Abby-Marie. "I'll go as long as you go with me, but you mustn't ever let go of me."

"I won't," said Lady Burd. "C'mon, let's go. We don't want to keep Edison waiting."

Abby-Marie gripped Lady Burd's hand, and they stepped out onto the deck. The sound of the helicopter was deafening, and the blast felt like they were walking through a hurricane.

"Close your eyes!" shouted Lady Burd. "I'll guide you to the basket!"

Abby-Marie couldn't decide which was worse, to see where she was going or to NOT see where she was going. She tightened her grip on Lady Burd's hand and tried a combination of the two. She squinted her eyes, allowing her to barely make out the tiny little face of Edison peering over the basket that was now dangling fifteen feet over the deck.

"Edison!" she shouted. "It's okay! We're coming for you!"

The little puppy heard Abby-Marie's voice and turned his head in her direction. At the same moment, a gust of wind forced the helicopter pilot to make a quick adjustment that shifted the basket and sent Edison falling to the deck below. The little Maltipoo landed on his back and started rolling toward the railing of the ship.

Abby-Marie screamed, "No! Theo!!!!"

"Theo?" wondered Lady Burd, "Who's Theo?" but she didn't have time to ask questions, she needed to act quickly. She was sure she could easily rescue the puppy if she had both of her hands free, but she had promised Abby-Marie she wouldn't let go of her.

"Hang on!" Lady Burd shouted, as she dove onto the deck dragging Abby-Marie behind her. They slammed to the ground and slid in Edison's direction. The little dog scratched its claws on the deck, trying to make it back to the girl he loved.

"Reach out your other hand!" shouted Lady Burd. Abby-Marie inched her way forward, extending her hand to grip the tiny paw of her furry friend. Her eyes were wide open now and filled with tears.

"I can't!" she shouted.

"Yes, you can!" responded Lady Burd confidently.

Abby-Marie took a final lunge and proved that Lady Burd was right. Her hand hooked one of Edison's tiny little toes, and she pulled him to her chest.

"Great work!" cheered Lady Burd. "C'mon now, let's get you guys back inside with the others!"

Hector the Inspector looked up and signaled to the helicopter pilot that all was clear. The military helicopter pulled up and away, disappearing into the bright blue sky. Suddenly, everything was calm and quiet.

"Hip, hip, hooray!" everyone cheered as Abby-Marie walked into the dining hall with Edison in her arms. "You're a hero!" shouted Lily.

"More like a ZERO!" Isabela whispered loudly enough that Abby-Marie could hear.

Abby-Marie knew she was right. She was a mess. Her whole body was shaking, her eyes were swollen and red from crying, and she was pretty sure she wet her pants just a little.

"Alright, everyone, settle down!" interrupted Dr. Tusen-Takk with the loudest voice she could muster. She had asked Dr. Donsky to bring her down to the dining hall once she regained consciousness.

"Mr. Hector has something to say on behalf of the Ecuadorian government," she said, calmly holding a large ice pack to her forehead.

"Well, all I can say…" Hector said, clearing his throat, "is that you must have friends in very high places!"
He stepped forward as if to give a very formal presentation.

"As I'm sure you all know, the Galápagos Islands represent one the world's most valuable treasures. This is a wildlife sanctuary, and quite honestly, to bring these dogs here is to put this sacred sanctuary at risk. Who knows all the diseases and germs they must carry!"

Professors Thomsen and Bloomfield had to work hard to keep from rolling their eyes. They both knew that the Wonder Doodles were easily some of the healthiest animals in the world.

"But somehow, you've managed to get clearance to bring them here," continued Hector the Inspector. "So let me be clear. This is against my wishes, but I will grant the Wonderwood Academy permission to conduct your school aboard this vessel under the following conditions:

1. No dog is ever to put one paw on the shore of these islands. The dogs are restricted to the ship and the sea.

2. The Wonderwood Academy is required to construct and maintain world-class boarding facilities, including kennels, aboard this ship.

3. You must always be prepared for surprise inspections. I reserve the right to board this ship at any time and without warning to make sure you are in compliance with the rules and regulations of my government.

If you fail to meet any of these requirements, we will be forced to ask you to leave the country!"

Hector clicked his heels to add authority and emphasis to his words. As he turned to leave, a large airhorn blasted from the water outside. Several emergency flares exploded off the bow.

"Oh, no," Dr. Tusen-Takk sighed, holding the ice pack to her forehead. "What now?"

5
THE EARTH PROTECTORS

Sven had just entered the dining hall with a large tray of snacks when another flare exploded.

Kaboom!

The Wonderwood Girls ran out on the deck and saw several small rubber boats circling below. People with green knitted caps, protest signs, and bullhorns were doing their best to make their feelings known.

"Wonderwood Academy, go home!" they shouted. "No dogs allowed! Wonderwood, go home!"

"It's the Earth Protecters!" said Nina. "Hector, did you let them know we were planning to bring the Wonder Doodles to the Galápagos?"

"Dogs are DOOM!" the protestors chanted over their bullhorns. "Dogs are DEATH!"

"¿*Estás loca*?" Hector replied. "Why would I want to make my life even more difficult? The less I'm forced to deal with these Earth Protector guys, the better!"

"Everyone keep calm!" exclaimed Nina to the girls and professors that joined her at the ship's railing. "We know most of these people. They're a group known as the Earth Protectors. They're not here to hurt us; they just don't understand our mission."

"What did we do?" asked Lily, looking up at Dr. Tusen-Takk.

"I guess they think our Wonder Doodles have canine diseases that could have serious effects on the wildlife here in the Galápagos," replied Dr. Tusen-Takk. "Nina, is there any way you can get Hector to call off these Earth Protectors? If they knew why we we're here, they wouldn't be protesting."

Dr. Nina Cruz pulled her brother aside. "Hector, there has to be something more important for these people to do."

"Well, I have received a few reports of an illegal fishing boat using nets to capture sea turtles and then selling them on the black market," he replied.

Hector walked over to the side of the ship and stepped over the railing. He descended a rope ladder so he could speak face to face with the angry protestors below. As soon as he said the word "turtle," the Earth Protectors put down their "DOGS ARE DEATH" signs and scrambled to find ones that read, "SAVE THE TURTLES!"

"I'll be back to check on the progress of those kennels!" shouted Hector. "Remember, failure to meet our conditions means you must leave!" Hector gave a sheepish smile and waved as he sailed off with the Earth Protectors in search of an illegal fishing boat and sea turtles in need of protection.

"Okay, everyone, so we're off to a rough start," said Dr. Tusen-Takk. "Why don't we go back to the dining hall and have a group meeting? Let's hit the reset button and start again, shall we? I don't think things could get much worse!"

But things were about to get worse. Much worse! A seagull with zombie eyes sat high above the deck perched on the ship's flagpole. The gull mechanically panned its head down toward the girls as they filed back into the dining hall. A miniature camera, planted in the seagull's skull captured the Wonderwood Girls' every move. The seagull waited until the last girl entered the dining hall and then flew away.

Thousands of miles away in a deep, hidden cave sat a man dressed in white surgical scrubs. He wore thick glasses, black rubber gloves, and a protective mask that covered his nose and mouth. "It looks like we need to kick things up a notch," he muttered under his breath.

The man was sitting in the Colossus Command Center, a cave filled with computer screens, joystick controls, keyboards, and buttons. He stared intensely at his screens. He was controlling a ship known as the SS Toothache, which was anchored just a few hundred yards away from the Seadoodle. Most notable, or perhaps most unnoticeable, was the fact that the ship was invisible. Colossus was using the same chameleon technology that the Wonderwood Academy used when privacy and secrecy were required. The only visible sign of the invisible ship's presence was the almost imperceptible heat vapor that drifted up into the air from the ship's engines.

Inside the invisible ship was a control room that received all the commands from the Colossus Command Center.

Behind the control room was a long, narrow cabin. The room was spotless. On either side were two long rows of oversized dentist chairs. Next to each of the chairs was a computer-controlled robot with several mechanical arms. At least four of these arms were designed for restraining, and the largest arms were designed to do things like squirting glue on fake teeth and performing implantations.

A warning buzzer sounded just as a long metal ramp descended into the water behind the ship. A conveyor belt whirled into motion as a pair of sea lions were pulled into the cabin. One of the sea lions had the same zombie stare as the spy-gull. The other looked like it was half asleep as it followed mindlessly behind. The man in the command center lifted a finger and laughed under his breath. "Time to start the procedure!"

The robot extended its arms to grab the sleepy sea lion. The robot easily lifted the 300-pound mammal and placed it onto the dentist chair. Wide leather straps surrounded the sea lion's chest, neck, and head. Two metal arms grabbed its upper and lower jaws and opened its mouth exposing two rows of teeth. Another arm scanned the sea lion's teeth, and determined its target. A fourth arm plunged the fake blue tooth into a jar of glue and firmly jammed it into the sea lion's mouth.

"Done!" exclaimed the man from the Colossus Command Center.

He pushed another button and the leather straps released. Instantly, the blue tooth inside the sea lion's mouth was activated, and the sea lion took on a blank expression like the other sea lion and seagull. The two sea lions climbed on the conveyor belt and were pulled back into the sea.

"My work is never done!" smiled the man, proud of his efforts. "Let's see now, that's over one hundred blue tooth implants this week!"

As the man gloated to himself he was startled as another man entered the room.

"Oh, hey, boss, what's up?" said the man seated at the controls.

"What's up?" the boss snapped. "I think your mission just might be up!" he growled with disappointment. "Why aren't the Wonderwood Girls leaving? You said they wouldn't be in the Galápagos more than a few hours!"

"Boss, c'mon, just relax! I'm starting with a more subtle approach. I thought the Earth Protectors would scare them away, but obviously these girls have some inside connections."

"Forget subtle approaches!" screamed the boss. "We've got too much at stake here. You hear me? Sink that Seadoodle if you have to. I want those Wonderwood Girls out of here!"

"Don't worry, boss. They'll all be gone before the week is over," he responded with a laugh. "I'll put a blue tooth in everyone of those girls if I have to. I'm The Dentist!"

6

LIFE AT SEA

Captain Carlos returned to the bridge and set a course for Beagle Bay. The rest of the team gathered in the dining hall for what they hoped would be the first of many uneventful meetings during the semester. Dr. Tusen-Takk stood and addressed the Wonderwood team.

"Let me begin by saying how proud I am of all of you," she began. "In the last twenty-four hours, we have seen our campus destroyed, endured an all-night flight to South America, and had our Wonder Doodles confiscated, only to be returned in a basket dangling from a helicopter. And now we have a group of protesters that has made it very clear they want us to leave."

Dr. Tusen-Takk lowered her head and tried to fight back the tears.

"Girls," she said trembling, "I'm tired....and my head hurts." She felt the swollen bump on her forehead. "I do wonder if we should just cancel school this year."

For the first time in days, Abby-Marie was excited. She wanted to raise her hand high. "I vote YES!" she screamed inside.

Instead, everyone else responded, "NO! We won't give up!"

Dr. Tusen-Takk was amazed by the strength and resilience of her Wonderwood Girls.

"You guys are amazing!" she said, taking courage from their enthusiasm.

"No, you're the one who is amazing!" said Sven as he walked to the front and put his arm around his cousin's shoulder. "I have something for you that I think will make your semester at sea a little more bearable." He pulled out an old ice hockey helmet from behind his back and placed it on her head. "We Norwegians are far too tall for ships like these," he said with a smile. "This helmet is the only thing that saved me when I first started working on cruise ships. I hope you like it."

All the girls, professors, and especially Lady Burd cheered.

"Well, it's not exactly what I would call a fashion statement," said Dr. Tusen-Takk in gratitude, "but if it keeps me out of the hospital, I think I can push my vanity aside. Okay, now let's begin."

The chancellor grabbed a stack of papers from the table and handed them out to the Wonderwood Girls and their professors.

"This handout shows a floor plan of the SS Seadoodle, our home for the next four months. If you look carefully, you will see that each of you will be sharing a cabin with the roommate we assigned to you last week. Professors, I'm sorry, but you too will need to share a cabin with one of your colleagues. Meals will be served at seven a.m., noon, and six p.m. Don't be late. Also…it's okay just for this meeting, but after this, no dogs in the dining hall or in your cabins. The Wonder Doodles will have to sleep on the deck until we can provide more suitable accommodations."

Dr. Tusen-Takk took a seat as she motioned to the professors to continue the presentation.

"Welcome everyone!" said Dr. Florence Khumalo, "I'm

excited to be teaching courses with Dr. Mitch Middletree this semester. Our area of expertise is language and culture. In my classes, we will focus especially on learning Latin American dances like the salsa, rumba, cha-cha, merengue, samba, and the tango!"

"And I will be teaching you to speak Spanish!" said Dr. Mitch Middletree with excitement. "Before the semester is over, you should be fairly fluent if you put in the effort."

Dr. Beth Broomfield and Dr. Brigitte Thomsen stood up next. "I'm sure you all know by now that our job is to work with the Wonder Doodles. We will work with you to build a home for them aboard this ship," said Dr. Thomsen.

"And…," Dr. Broomfield added. "We really want to see if these guys can work well underwater! I think our dogs are natural swimmers, and I can't wait to see if we can teach our doodles to scuba dive!"

Dr. Maggie Middletree and Dr. Kyoto Matsura stood next. "Our job," said Dr. Middletree, "is to develop new technologies that will assist our research underwater. We want to give you girls the power to stay underwater longer so you can advance our research and get more done."

"And why do we want to stay underwater longer?" asked Dr. Esti Yaron as she stood with her colleague Dr. Maribel Martinez. "So, we can spend more time harvesting our underwater crops!"

"That's right," added Dr. Martinez. "The Cruz family has been working for many years with the concept of underwater farming, and we're here to help them take seaweed farming to the next level."

"Seaweed?" asked Evie Kron. "Yuck!"

"You might think that seaweed is unpleasant," jumped in Dr. Bibi Bouchon, "but Dr. Olga Donsky and I are convinced that it will be the next big thing in nutrition and culinary innovation. We will be working with Sven to see how we can make seaweed a part of our daily menu. Stay tuned!"

"It's disgusting!" protested Isabela. "I hate seaweed. It's slimy and green. It stinks, it's worthless, and besides, I think I'm allergic to it!"

"Worthless?" countered Dr. Esti Yaron. "I believe that's the very thing I would like to disprove."

"Well, this all sounds wonderful," interrupted Lady Burd, "but we won't be here at all if we don't get this ship set up with state-of-the-art kennels to make a home for our furry friends!"

Everyone nodded.

"Hector the Inspector will be 'hounding' us, pun intended," laughed Lady Burd. "Yes, he'll be hounding us until we convince him that the doodles are no threat to the wildlife around us."

"I agree," said Dr. Tusen-Takk. "Until the rooms for the doodles are ready, we're in jeopardy of getting sent home. The kennels are our highest priority. Let's get to work!"

The sun was shining warmly on the water as the SS Seadoodle arrived at Beagle Bay. Captain Carlos lowered the anchor as a small pod of dolphins played together just a few yards away. All the girls rushed to the railing to get a better look. As Anna Andersen joined the other girls at the railing she glanced down at the surface below her feet.

"Is this deck made of what I think it is?" asked Anna, looking curiously at the entire surface of the ship.

"I was wondering when you would notice," said Lady Burd. "Yes, it's the same material we use on the roads at the Wonderwood Academy back home."

"Does that mean we can use our Wonder Discs here?" Anna asked, trying hard not to show her excitement.

"Too bad we didn't bring them," replied Lady Burd with a sly grin as she glanced over at a large wooden crate on the deck.

"Really?" Anna cheered as she reached to pry open the top of the large box. "Ruth, Grace, check this out! It's our Wonder Discs!"

Anna dug through the discs, looking for the one with her name on it. She pulled it out and activated it with her ring.

"Stand back, girls," Anna shouted as she hopped onto her disc and made a quick lap around the deck. "But wait for it… wait for it… here it comes!" she screamed as she flew past the group. "Here's the big finish!" She jumped from her disc, flew over the ship's railing, and plunged into the water below clothes and all.

"Whoa! What was that?" shouted Lily.

"I don't know," laughed Ruth, "but I want to try it too!"

Ruth, Grace, Isabela, Mikako, and Evie all scrambled to grab their Wonder Discs from the crate.

"I'm next!" shouted Isabela. "It's my parents' boat, so I'm next!"

"Is this allowed?" asked Faith, staring at Lady Burd in disbelief.

"It sure looks like fun to me!" said Lady Burd as she started looking through the box for her own Wonder Disc.

"Well, I don't think it's for me," said Lily looking back at Abby-Marie and the younger girls, Faith and Natasha, for support.

Dr. Tusen-Takk could see that some of the girls who weren't swimming were uncomfortable, so she stepped out onto the deck carrying several large boxes, "Girls would you like to help me sort out our new school uniforms?"

"We have new uniforms?" ask Nati. "Let's try them on!" she squealed as she rushed back into the dining hall.

The four girls returned with their new uniforms and pretended to be fashion models on a runway.

Lily narrated the scene: "And sporting our new 'summer at sea' collection, we have the amazing seafaring Wonderwood Girls. As you can see, the girls are wearing a cotton blend t-shirt boasting our school colors and crest. The color-coordinated shorts they're wearing are made of a polyester blend for added comfort and flexibility. Their shoes are the world's finest deck shoes, with leather uppers and rubber soles."

"Great fashion show!" said Lady Burd as she climbed back on deck dripping wet from her swim in the bay. She turned back to the other girls who were still in the water below. "Okay, girls, time to wrap this up. Let's dry off and get you into your new uniforms. I want you guys looking keen and sharp like these four girls standing before us!"

"You mean the girls who are too afraid to fly?" Isabela whispered under her breath as she passed Abby-Marie and the other girls. Abby-Marie frowned and dropped her head.

"Don't let her bother you," said Lily. "She's just putting on a show."

Abby-Marie started trembling in anger and blurted, "I think it's time Isabela's show got canceled!"

7

SAUSAGE AND CIPHERS

"I love it here!" said Grace.

"Me too!" added her sister, Ruth. "Especially after that amazing swim in the ocean!"

"Well, that's good to hear," said Mitch Middletree as he approached his daughters with two large traveling cases. "Do you think you could call Evie and Natasha over here too? I have a special assignment, and I think you four girls are perfect for the job!"

"*Hola*, Dr. Middletree!" said Evie as she walked up with her roommate, Natasha. "What's in the cases?"

"Evie, how would you like to make a film?" asked Dr. Middletree as he pulled a camera from one of the cases. "I think you would make an excellent director."

"Well…urh… ummm," Evie stammered.

"Grace, would you be the producer?" he asked. "Ruth, I want you to operate the camera. And Nati, would you oversee the lighting and sound? I will be the executive producer of course, but I would certainly give you girls lots of creative control over style and content."

"What would the film be about?" asked Natasha.

"I want you to produce a documentary film. You know, like for National Geographic or the Discovery Channel. I think it's important to have a digital record of our semester at sea. What do you girls think? Are you up for it?"

"I guess so," replied Grace, "but where do we start?"

"Wow, great question!" responded Dr. Middletree. "I wish we had time for me to teach a whole course on documentary filmmaking this semester, but I think you just showed me that you already know the answer to your question."

"I did?"

"Yep, you asked a great question! That's the secret to making an award-winning documentary film."

"Ask questions?"

"Not just questions, GREAT questions!" Dr. Middletree responded. "You need to find out what's going on in people's hearts. Audiences want to know about people's hopes, fascinations, and fears!"

"My fear is that I'm going to make a terrible film!" said Evie.

"Don't worry," said Dr. Middletree. "Just start by getting to know your camera equipment. Do some short interviews, and I'll review the footage with you at the end of every day. You'll be pros in no time!"

"Great," Grace replied. "Let's go down to our cabin so we can put together a plan!"

It didn't take the four girls long to figure out just how tiny their cabins were. They sat knee to knee on two narrow beds that filled over half the room. There was a single porthole that let in light and gave some indication of the weather conditions outside. Each cabin had a private bathroom, but the toilet, sink, and shower were all crammed into the space of a small closet.

"I say we get out of here!" said Ruth. "Let's go back on deck and see if we can go swimming again!"

"No," countered Grace. "Let's do what Dad said. Let's start by doing some simple interviews!"

"Okay," said Evie, "but who do you want to interview first?"

"Why not Sven?" said Natasha. "He seems pretty interesting."

"Sounds good to me," said Ruth. "Although he does seem to be missing some hair from his moustache!"

The girls figured out how to connect the battery and microphone. Natasha put on headphones to monitor the audio, and Ruth powered up the camera. The four young filmmakers walked down the corridor to find Sven.

"May we come in?" Grace asked, knocking on the door of the ship's cooking galley.

"Who's there?" Sven responded without looking up. He was chopping vegetables and didn't want to risk slicing a finger.

"We're the Wonderwood Academy film crew!" replied Grace. "We were hoping to ask you a few questions."

"Do I have to?" said Sven reluctantly.

"Pleeeeeease!" begged the four girls in unison.

"We chose you to be our first interview!" added Grace.

"Okay, but it can't take too long. I have to get dinner ready for you girls!"

Evie entered the room and started working with Ruth to determine the best angle for the camera.

"Let's put the camera here," she said. "This angle gets all those pots and pans in the background and these beautiful, chopped vegetables in the foreground."

Sven put down his knife and took a seat behind the preparation table. He adjusted his apron and repositioned the chef hat on his bald head.

"What's the first question?"

"Oh, you know, questions like what's your name, how old are you, where were you born?" answered Grace.

"Ask him why he showed up here carrying a box with

the Colossus logo on it!" interrupted Natasha.

"Wow—sounds like there's some emotion behind that question," Sven responded.

"I'm sorry," Grace said with embarrassment. "I'll ask another question."

"No, I'm happy to answer that one," Sven answered confidently. "I found that box on my old cruise ship. The cruise line I worked for used to buy food products from Colossus. Nasty stuff, but I needed an empty box to carry my meat grinder, so I took it."

"Meat grinder?" asked Grace curious to know more.

"As a chef, I'm fascinated with sausage making!" he grinned. "There's an endless combination of delicacies you can make in the wonderful and fascinating world of encased meats!"

"Endless?" Grace raised an eyebrow.

"Yes, endless," Sven said. "Think about it. You can grind up anything, pork, beef, chicken. And, you can add any spice to the combination. Something tells me your professors are going to have me adding seaweed before too long."

"Ask him what happened to his moustache," smiled Ruth.

"And why he doesn't have any hair," added Evie.

"Or who's the woman in that picture on the wall? Are you in love?" asked Natasha.

Sven turned red.

"C'mon, girls," said Grace. "Give the man a break!" Grace looked around the kitchen and noticed a small book with worn pages next to Sven's radio. "Is that book a collection of all your secret recipes?"

"Actually," replied Sven, "it's my collection of secret codes and ciphers. I have two hobbies: the first is sausage making, and the second is collecting ways to hide messages and keep secret information."

"Do you have lots of secrets to keep?" asked Grace.

"No," responded Sven, "but there's lots of people out there who do. Let me give you an example."

Sven grabbed the radio from the counter and switched it on.

"I found this radio station just a few hours ago. They

play classic rock in English. I love the music, but something isn't right. Do you hear that static noise in the background? It's not part of the radio signal; it's something different. That noise has a purpose. People have been hiding messages in audio recordings for decades, and I'm pretty sure that static is more than just noise. Someone is transmitting a secret message!"

8

THE SOUTHERN CROSS

Everyone agreed that Sven's cooking was truly amazing. In the short time he had to make dinner, he managed to bake fresh bread and prepare a colorful pasta primavera that looked like a work of art.

"I could get used to this!" said Mikako as she plunged her fork into the chocolate chip cookie sundae Sven had prepared for dessert.

"Yes, thank you, cousin!" added Dr. Tusen-Takk. "I think you're going to make it very difficult for me to get these girls to eat our cafeteria food back home."

"I would consider myself a failure if I didn't," he replied, tapping the hockey helmet on his cousin's head with a spoon. "I'll make sure these girls get fed, and you make sure to protect your noggin!"

Dr. Martinez, who was sitting across the table from Dr. Tusen-Takk, cleared her throat and stood to her feet. "Dr. T, would you mind if I excused myself? I need to check on the mini subs with Dr. Yaron, and then I think I'm going to make it an early night and get to bed. We have a big day tomorrow."

"I think that's wise," Dr. Tusen-Takk responded as she turned to address the group. "Girls, I want you all to get to bed early tonight. We have a surprise for you tomorrow, and you all need to be at your very best. Remember, breakfast is at seven o'clock sharp!"

The girls cleared the dishes and wiped down the tables. Five girls helped Sven wash the pots and pans, and the other five set the tables for breakfast the next morning.

"I could get used to this!" Sven smiled.

"Count on it," said Ruth. "We're the Wonderwood Girls! And, Sven, we've got your back too!"

The ten girls filed out of the dining hall and made their

way to their cabins. They immediately pulled out their pajamas and brushed their teeth. Lily and Abby-Marie fluffed their pillows and pulled their blankets up tight around their necks. Lily tried to sleep, but she couldn't. She lay in bed staring at the ceiling listening to Abby-Marie snore.

"I can't do it!" she declared under her breath. "I can't sleep knowing that Cousteau is out there on the deck with a broken leg!"

Lily grabbed her pillow, blanket, and thin mattress and made her way outside to the main deck, where Dr. Broomfield and Dr. Thomsen had made a place for the Wonder Doodles to sleep.

"Hello, boy," she said hugging Cousteau around the neck. "Would you mind some company?" She put down her mattress and made her bed beside him.

"Is it alright if I join you guys?" said Faith, trying not to startle her friend. "I missed my doodle too."

Next came Natasha, then Anna and Mikako. It wasn't long before all the Wonderwood Girls were set up to spend the night sleeping out on the deck with their doodles. Everyone except for Abby-Marie.

"I think I'm going back to my cabin and wake up my

roommate," said Lily. "I would hate for her to miss this."

"Oh, just let her sleep!" said Isabela, "She's no fun anyway."

Lily knew better than to listen to Isabela. "We're a team," said Lily, "and she needs to be with us."

"Yes, we're a team," said Grace, "and I think we need to film this! Ruth, let's get the camera and do some interviews."

The two girls followed Lily below and quickly returned with their microphone and camera. The air was fresh, and the bay was calm. Tiny waves gently rocked the Seadoodle on the surface of the water.

"Isabela, let's start with you," Grace stretched out the microphone in Isabela's direction. "What's it like to be back here in the Galápagos with your family aboard this amazing ship?"

Isabela was about to answer when Abby-Marie arrived with Lily and Lady Burd.

"Anyone up for s'mores?" interrupted Lady Burd.

Lady Burd opened a box that contained marshmallows, Ecuadorian chocolate, graham crackers, and some short wooden skewers. "You won't believe it, but Sven thought of everything! Look what I found in the kitchen," she said, raising a bag of marshmallows and handful of large wax candles.

"Promise me you won't burn down the ship!" ordered Lady Burd with a smile. "It's not the same as having a campfire, but I think these candles will toast up a marshmallow just fine."

"What's all the commotion?" asked Mitch Middletree as he and his wife, Maggie, joined the growing group.

"We went to check on you girls and found your cabin empty," said Maggie.

"Sorry, Mom," said Ruth. "We all wanted to be with our doodles, so we decided to sleep out here underneath the stars!"

"Speaking of stars," said Lady Burd, "have you had a chance to look at the sky above us?"

The girls laid back on their mattresses and let out a collective gasp, "Whoa! That's amazing!"

"*Meditare Miraculum*," Lady Burd whispered the school motto. "Isn't the night sky filled with wonder? Do you girls recognize any of these constellations?"

"Most of us have never seen the stars in the Southern Hemisphere," said Dr. Mitch. "Aren't they amazing? Do you see those four stars over there? That's the Southern Cross!"

"And that bright star over there is Alpha Centuari," said Maggie. "It would be great to see it through a telescope!"

Lady Burd sat down on the deck next to Abby-Marie, who was quietly holding her Maltipoo, Edison.

"How are you doing, Abby-Marie?" she asked, reaching down to pet Edison's soft furry back. "It's nice to have your friend back, isn't it?"

"I think I'm a little homesick," Abby-Marie said quietly, and then she coughed as if something was caught in her throat. "There's something else that's bothering me too, but I don't know how to talk about it."

"Does it have to do with someone named Theo?" asked Lady Burd gently, remembering the name Abby-Marie had cried out.

Abby-Marie froze. "How did you kno…."

"It's okay, we don't have to," said Lady Burd reassuringly.

"No, I want to, but not now… I'm not ready. Do you think I could come visit you sometime?"

"Of course," said Lady Burd. "Come to my cabin anytime. I'll make some tea."

As Lady Burd finished her invitation, a seagull glided down from the night sky and landed on the flagpole.

Mitch Middletree noticed the bird and pointed it out to the group.

"Hey, everyone, do you see that seagull? That reminds me of a little-known scientific fact. Do you know why seagulls don't fly over the bay?" he paused for dramatic effect. "Because then they would be 'bay-gulls.' Get it? Bagels! Hey, Ruth…" he motioned to his daughter, "bring that camera over here. Let's get that joke on camera. I think it's hilarious."

Grace groaned, "No, Dad, we're not putting any of your jokes in the movie!"

The seagull mechanically turned its head toward Grace as a tiny camera attached to its head slowly zoomed in.

"That's right, girls, make your cute little movie," said the man with the thick glasses and rubber gloves. "Eat s'mores, eat chocolate, get cavities. It won't be long before it's time for you to take a trip to The Dentist!"

9

AQUADOODLES

"Rise and shine!" shouted Dr. Martinez as she passed through the rows of sleeping girls on the ship's deck. "Don't make me get out a bucket of water!"

"Where am I?" yawned Faith as she sat up and wiped the sleep from her eyes.

"We're in paradise!" said Isabela with a voice that was far too cheery for the morning.

On the other end of the deck, a crane with a long arm and thick steel cable came to life as Captain Carlos switched on the controls and began lowering large wooden crates onto the deck below.

"What's in those big crates?" asked Ruth.

"A surprise!" said Dr. Martinez, eager to share her secret. "I need you to get your blankets and things back to your cabin, eat breakfast, and then meet me back here on deck by at eight o'clock sharp."

"Aye, aye, captain!" said Anna as she saluted her young professor. "I hope your surprise has something to do with exploring underwater!"

"It just might," grinned Dr. Martinez. "Don't be late!"

After breakfast, the Wonderwood Girls talked excitedly as they made their way to the rear deck at the end of the ship.

"This is awesome!" Everyone screamed except Abby-Marie. Before them was a small fleet of mini submarines parked in rows like cars in a parking lot.

Dr. Maggie Middletree stepped up and laid a gentle hand on the outer shell of one of the submarines. "Ladies, I am proud to announce that because of a generous donation from the Cochrane Foundation, we don't have one research submarine to use this semester, we have twelve Aquadoodles!"

Everyone cheered as they all secretly tried to calculate in their heads how much money you would need to purchase twelve submarines.

"That means you girls will be going on underwater excursions as a group!" added Dr. Matsura with pride. "Our surprise this morning is that Dr. Martinez and Dr. Yaron will be taking you on a guided tour of our seaweed farm."

The girls tried to cheer, but Dr. Martinez interrupted, "Hold on everyone! First, we need to do some serious training. These submarines are not toys!"

"Yes, that's right," added Dr. Yaron. "These subs may look small and cute, but they are extremely powerful. The propellor on each one of these has so much force that it is capable of ripping through the hull of a ship!"

"So, listen up and watch carefully," said Dr. Martinez as she slipped inside one of the subs. "I'm going to switch on the sub's intercom system, so you can all hear me. All the Aquadoodles have an intercom system, so we can communicate with one another while we're exploring underwater. Just remember not to all talk at once. It's best to keep quiet and let us do most of the talking when we're down there."

Abby-Marie looked over at Isabela, "Yeah, let the professors do the talking!"

"These submarines are really simple to operate," continued Dr. Martinez as she grasped the steering wheel in front of her. "This single steering control is all you really need to know for now. You push it forward, you go forward. The further you push, the faster you go. Pull it backward, and you guessed it, you go backward. Turn it to the right, you go right—left, you go left. Lift it up, you ascend, push it down, and you head toward the ocean floor."

"And what's that button in the middle?" asked Evie. "Is that the underwater horn?"

"Funny," answered Dr. Martinez. "No, that's the stabilizer button. It's like parking your submarine. No matter where you are in the water, when you press it, the submarine will maintain that position. It allows you to observe and work without having to worry about the ocean current carrying you away."

"And what about those glove control things?" asked Grace.

"We'll get to those a little bit later," replied Dr. Martinez. "Eventually, we'll use those glove controls to operate the harvesting tools attached to the front of the submarine. For now, let's just concentrate on driving the sub and getting back to the ship safely. Are you girls ready?"

Abby-Marie certainly was not. "No," she whispered under her breath.

"C'mon, Frenchie!" said Lily to her roommate grabbing her arm and pulling her toward the subs. "I've got your back."

Reluctantly, Abby-Marie climbed into her submarine as Lily closed the clear domed hatch over her head. One by one, Captain Cruz attached his cable to each submarine and gently lowered it into the water. Once all the girls were in the water and sitting at the controls of their mini subs, Dr. Martinez switched on the intercom once again.

"Okay everyone, follow my instructions! We're going to play a simple game of Follow the Leader. I'm the leader, and I want you all to follow me in a single-file line. When I descend, you descend. When I turn, you turn. Got it?"

"Got it!" said Anna, eager to get going.

"Dr. Yaron will be bringing up the rear. If any of you are having trouble, just let her know and she will come along to assist you. Remember to keep calm, and don't panic!"

As the group started out on their tour and the controls became second nature, everyone paused to take in the magic of the moment. The bottom half of each tiny sub was made of blue stainless steel, while the upper half was made of thick acrylic that looked like glass. It was like sitting inside a bubble with the underwater world in clear sight all around. The sun was streaming through the water from the surface above, and large schools of fish moved in unison as the girls floated past.

"It looks like we're not the only school in the ocean," joked Lily as several hundred silver fish changed course in front of her.

"Yes," said Dr. Yaron, "And it's about time for our school to begin its first session."

Dr. Martinez led the group to a large wall of green plant life floating in long rows, with each plant extending from the water's surface to the sea floor below.

"Did you know that there are over twelve thousand species of seaweed?" began Dr. Yaron. "We're only beginning to find out the unlimited potential of this amazing plant! In this underwater farm, we have over one hundred different varieties, and our hope is that you girls will help discover all the different things they can do."

"Just don't make us eat it!" interrupted Isabela.

"Well, my goal is to change your mind about that!" Dr. Yaron defended. "I think you'll be begging for it for breakfast, lunch, and dinner once we get our recipes perfected!"

Dr. Yaron's Aquadoodle jumped forward with the emotion of her words. The front end of her submarine entered the first row of green plants, and she got slightly tangled in the seaweed stalks in front of her.

"Oops! That reminds me," said Dr. Yaron. "Be careful not to steer your submarines into the seaweed. You could slice up our crops and do a lot of damage."

As Dr. Yaron finished saying the word "damage," everyone noticed that a small section of seaweed started to thrash violently back and forth in the water.

"Look!" shouted Ruth over the intercom. "Something's caught in the seaweed!"

10
SEAWEED RESCUE

Ruth guided her Aquadoodle into position so she could get a better look.

"There's too much seaweed!" she reported over the intercom. "Whatever it is, they've gotten themselves all tangled up in a giant ball of seaweed!"

The thrashing continued as the creature inside struggled for its life.

"Let me give it a try," said Dr. Martinez as she positioned her Aquadoodle just a few feet above Ruth's mini submarine.

"Now, Ruth, if you can lower your sub a few feet, I think I can float in over the top of you and begin cutting away some of that seaweed with these harvesting tools."

Dr. Martinez glided into position and quickly pushed the stabilizer button to steady her craft. She inserted her hands into the glove controls on either side of the steering wheel and then moved her left hand to extend a harvesting arm to grab a clump of seaweed. With the other robot arm she started cutting seaweed.

"Well, take a look at this!" said Dr. Martinez. "It's a baby sea turtle!"

It was hard for everyone to see, but the head of a cute baby sea turtle was struggling to push its way out from the large wad of seaweed.

"Move aside!" commanded Isabela, forcing her way past the other girls. "I need to get in there!"

The twelve Aquadoodles were all crammed together hovering at the edge of the underwater farm about twenty feet below the surface. It looked like an underwater traffic jam.

"Careful to give each other space to maneuver!" cautioned Dr. Yaron. "Remember, those propellors can cut through steel. We don't want to you guys to slice a chunk out of your Aquadoodles!"

"Yeah, give me some space!" shouted Isabela, struggling to push past Lily, Natasha, and Abby-Marie.

"Hey, be careful!" shouted Lily as Isabela's mini sub pushed Lily out of the way like a bumper car.

"I think I need to be here more than you do!" scolded Isabela. "Now back off!"

Isabela skillfully guided her sub into position next to Ruth and Dr. Martinez.

"What's the plan?" Isabela asked Dr. Martinez as if she had been rescuing sea turtles her whole life.

"We have to free this turtle fast!" said Dr. Martinez. "Sea turtles can hold their breath for a long time, but they can't stay underwater forever!"

Isabela pressed the stabilizer button and slipped her hands into the remote-control gloves. She extended her right hand to pull back some more seaweed, but instead the mechanical arm caught hold of a thick rope. As she pulled, some of the seaweed gave way and revealed the true source of the problem.

"It's a fishing net!" cried Ruth. "That illegal fishing boat Inspector Hector was talking about must have trapped this little guy, and somehow it escaped!"

"Well, we need to move quickly! I'm afraid if we don't get this turtle to the surface, it's going to drown!" said Dr. Martinez as she stood in her sub and started looking under the seat and the compartment behind her.

"We need to cut that net now!"

Dr. Martinez found what she was looking for. In the emergency compartment was a small scuba tank, diving mask, fins, and a large diver's knife.

"Quick! Ruth, Anna, Isabela, stabilize your Aquadoodles and grab the scuba gear from the back of your sub. Slip though the escape hatch and join me in the water!"

The three girls sprang into action. They quickly strapped on their scuba tanks, descended through the escape hatch, and swam to meet Dr. Martinez in the water outside their submarines. The four divers surrounded the large ball of seaweed and grabbed the fishing net. Dr. Martinez pulled out her knife as she motioned to the girls to start cutting at the net from all sides. The girls started hacking away at the net while trying to keep the turtle calm as they pulled off chunks of seaweed. Dr. Martinez took the regulator from her mouth and tried to force air into the turtle's nostrils, hoping to fill its empty lungs. Finally, the turtle broke free and swam to the surface. The girls followed the turtle to the open air above them.

"Wow, that was intense!" shouted Anna as she broke the surface.

They circled the small sea turtle, who was gasping for air and exhausted from the struggle.

"Looks like a female," said Dr. Martinez. "My guess is she didn't have much time left. Girls, I think we saved this little turtle's life!"

"She doesn't look like she's in very good shape," said Ruth, pulling the regulator from her mouth. "And what's with this tooth? It's blue!"

"Tooth?" said Dr. Martinez. "Turtles don't have teeth, and they're certainly not blue!"

Suddenly, as if a switch had been turned on, the turtle's body turned stiff, and her eyes took on a zombie-like stare.

"What's going on?" said Isabela.

"I don't know," said Dr. Martinez. "I've never seen a

turtle behave this way before."

The small turtle seemed to regain its strength, and it started moving its flipper in an attempt to break free from the girls and make its way to the island behind them.

"It's free!" said Anna.

"And alive," said Dr. Martinez. "We've done all we can. Let's get back to our subs and finish that tour!"

The four of them put their regulators back in their mouths and plunged into the water and swam back down to their submarines just twenty feet below.

"Well, that was interesting!" Dr. Martinez reported to the group once she was safely back into the seat of her Aquadoodle.

"What happened?" asked Faith, who was in the back of the group. "I couldn't see anything!"

"We rescued a small female sea turtle!" reported Dr. Martinez. "It was about to drown, so I asked Ruth, Anna, and Isabela to help me cut her free."

"I think we should call her Shellie," said Natasha.

"Cute," said Dr. Yaron. "I hope we all get to see her again. Now, why don't we finish our tour and get back to the Seadoodle so we can have some lunch? Anyone hungry?"

"I am!" shouted Isabela as she stowed her scuba tank and took back the controls of her sub. "Let's get going!"

Isabela turned her mini sub around and crashed right into the back of Abby-Marie.

"Don't you know how to drive?" scolded Isabela.

"It won't go!" replied Abby-Marie.

"Yes, it will!" yelled Isabela impatiently. "Let me help you!"

Isabela jammed her steering wheel forward and slammed again into the back of Abby-Marie's Aquadoodle. The impact forced Abby-Marie's head and body forward, causing her submarine to jolt out of control.

"I think this puts a whole new meaning to on the phrase, 'I've got your back,'" laughed Isabela as she slammed again into the back of Abby-Marie's submarine.

Abby-Marie's face went white with fear as the jolt sent her out to sea. All she could do was scream.

"Help!!!"

11

I'VE GOT YOUR BACK

Abby-Marie's worst nightmare was coming true. Her knuckles turned white as she gripped the steering wheel with all her might. She couldn't move. She was frozen with fear.

"Pull back!" shouted Dr. Martinez. "Pull back on the wheel!"

Abby-Marie was helpless. Her fear turned to panic, and her panic to shock!

"Don't, Theo!" she whispered. "Don't!"

The powerful propellor of her submarine churned into high gear and quickly reached top speed. It was less than three seconds before she disappeared into deep water.

"Quick girls, follow her!" ordered Dr. Martinez

The young professor was living her own worst nightmare. One of her students was in serious danger. She knew the mini subs had a limited supply of air, and she calculated they had less than thirty minutes to find Abby-Marie before her oxygen would run out.

"Spread out girls!" Dr. Martinez ordered. "First one to find Abby-Marie sends me her location. Got it? I'll join you as fast as I can!"

Anna, Ruth, and Isabela didn't hesitate and immediately disappeared in pursuit.

"I'm scared!" said Faith over the intercom.

"Me too," added Lily.

"You girls stick with me!" said Dr. Yaron. "We can look for Abby-Marie together!"

Natasha also decided to stay behind with Dr. Yaron, but Evie, Grace, and Mikako followed Dr. Martinez to help find their friend.

Abby-Marie was now unconscious. Her forehead had smashed against the glass and was starting to bleed. Her body was slumped over the steering wheel, which only made her submarine go faster. Seaweed tangled several times around the submarine's arms and propellor, which forced it to crash to the ocean floor. Abby-Marie smashed into a coral reef, which flipped her submarine upside down. The small craft came to a stop as her body fell off the steering wheel and landed on the glass, which was now resting on the sandy bottom of the ocean floor. A small crack formed, and her cockpit started to fill with water.

"Any sign of Abby-Marie?" Dr. Martinez asked the girls over the intercom.

"No, nothing!" responded Isabela. "No, wait. I see something!"

Isabela looked down and saw tiny bubbles escaping from Abby-Marie's capsized submarine directly below her.

"Your location!" shouted Dr. Martinez. "I need your location!"

Isabela immediately descended, ignoring the command. She saw Abby-Marie lying unconscious in the cockpit of her sub that was rapidly filling with water.

"I have to get her out of there!" shouted Isabela. "I'm going in!"

"No, wait for me!" ordered Dr. Martinez. "Send me your location!"

"No time," said Isabela as she put on her diving mask and slipped into the water through the escape hatch.

Isabela swam down to Abby-Marie's sub and tapped on the glass, trying to get her to regain consciousness. Abby-Marie didn't respond. Isabela then swam to the escape hatch and opened it. Water immediately filled the cockpit and Abby-Marie's body started to float. Isabela grabbed her classmate's ankle and pulled her through the escape hatch. She placed her arm around Abby-Marie's waist and kicked as hard as she could to reach the surface.

As the two girls emerged out of the water, Isabela ripped the regulator from her own mouth and shouted, "C'mon, little French girl! You can make it!"

Isabela leaned Abby-Marie's body back in the water; she tilted back her head and started giving Abby-Marie mouth-to-mouth.

"C'mon now, breathe!" she scolded as she filled the motionless girl's lungs with air.

Nothing. No movement. Abby-Marie was gone.

"No! You can't die on me!" screamed Isabela.

Isabela pressed her lips to Abby-Marie's mouth and gave one last blast of air to fill her lungs.

"You can't die! Can't you see I've got your back?"

In desperation, Isabela slapped Abby-Marie's face. Suddenly, a gurgling sound escaped from Abby-Marie's throat and enormous amounts of sea water erupted from her mouth. Abby-Marie opened her eyes and instantly slapped Isabela in the face as if to return the favor.

"You've got my back?!? You've got my back?!?" Abby-Marie gasped in disbelief. "Last I knew you were ramming me in the back with your submarine!"

In less than a minute, Dr. Martinez and the rest of the Wonderwood Girls arrived to find the two girls floating in the water.

"Why didn't you answer me?" scolded Dr. Martinez.

"I didn't have time!" Isabela protested. "I thought she

was going to drown."

"We'll talk about this later!" Dr. Martinez responded, trying to hide her anger. "Right now, we must get Abby-Marie into my sub and back to the Seadoodle! We also need to get that damaged submarine off the ocean floor and back to the ship for repairs."

"I think Anna and I can get that sub back to the surface," Ruth said confidently.

"And I can help!" Isabela added.

"Oh no you don't, young lady!" said Dr. Martinez. "You're coming back with me. You and I need to have a long talk."

"We're down to about ten to fifteen minutes of air," interrupted Dr. Yaron. "I'm going to bring the rest of the girls back to the Seadoodle by cruising on the surface."

"That's fine," replied Dr. Martinez, "but that will take twice as long. I need to get Abby-Marie back to the ship as quickly as possible."

Dr. Martinez flipped a switch and opened the glass dome of her submarine. "Slide Abby-Marie over here, and I'll get her back to the ship. The rest of you start making your way back to the Seadoodle with Dr. Yaron," ordered Dr. Martinez. "Ruth and Anna, bring Abby-Marie's sub to the surface and tow it back slowly. I don't want it filling up with water on the way back."

"And me?" asked Isabela. "What do you want me to do?"

"You?" said Dr. Martinez. "You?!? I want you to keep quiet and get ready to defend your actions! I'm calling for a tribunal."

12

FACING THE CONSEQUENCES

It took Ruth and Anna more than an hour to get Abby-Marie's Aquadoodle back to the surface. The two girls used a scuba tank to fill the damaged cockpit with air, forcing out the water and eventually causing the submarine to float back to the surface.

"Whoever crashed this submarine is lucky to be alive!" said Captain Cruz as a crane pulled the mangled mini sub from the water and lowered it onto the deck. "I'm glad Isabela was there to come to her rescue."

"Well, there's a little more to the story," interrupted Dr. Martinez. "C'mon, everyone. Dr. Tusen-Takk wants us all to meet in the dining hall to discuss what just happened!"

Dr. Tusen-Takk pulled Lady Burd aside. "I think Abby-Marie needs to get some rest. What we need to discuss here is only going to make things worse for her. Would you mind taking her down to her cabin? I think you should stay with her and make sure she's okay."

Lady Burd nodded, reaching out to take Abby-Marie's hand. "C'mon, girl, let's get you down to your room and into dry clothes."

In less than ten minutes, the tribunal proceedings began as everyone took their seats in the dining hall.

"Everyone, let's come to order, declared Dr. Tusen-Takk. "This tribunal is now in session!" Dr. Olga Donsky stood with the Wonderwood Academy rulebook in her hand.

"It grieves me that Dr. Martinez has requested this tribunal hearing," Dr. Donsky began. "This is only our second day in the Galápagos, and already we are forced to take formal disciplinary action."

Dr. Donsky motioned to Isabela and pointed to a spot on the floor next to her. Isabela stood, took her place, then lowered her head in shame.

"Representing the Wonderwood Academy will be Dr. Maribel Martinez," Dr. Donsky began. "Isabela, which faculty member would you like to defend you?"

"Can I choose my mother?" asked Isabela.

Dr. Donsky looked over to Dr. Tusen-Takk, who nodded, giving her approval.

"Okay, then let the proceedings begin."

Dr. Donsky opened the rule book and began the accusation. "From the facts that we've been told, it appears that Isabela Cruz is guilty of breaking three rules:

1. FIGHTING,
2. DAMAGING PRIVATE PROPERTY,
3. DISGRACEFUL BEHAVIOR.

Dr. Martinez, would you please state your case?"

Dr. Martinez stood and attempted to give her testimony without emotion, but she couldn't hide her anger. "I told Isabela several times to give me her location. She refused. I told her to wait for me to arrive before beginning the rescue. She took matters into her own hands!"

Dr. Nina Cruz stood next. "Isabela was born on the Galápagos Islands; she has lived here her whole life. She was scuba diving at age eight, learned to operate a mini sub at nine, and was certified as a search and rescue diver at age ten! We taught her to do exactly what she did today, and Abby-Marie is alive because of her!"

"And Abby-Marie could also be dead because of her!" Dr. Martinez steamed. "We were lucky today. But this never would have happened if Isabela wasn't so bossy and impatient. She was being a bully!"

"Is this true?" Dr. Cruz asked as she looked down to make eye contact with her daughter.

"It is!" shouted Lily from the back of the room. "We all feel it!"

"Order!" snapped Dr. Donsky. "The tribunal has not recognized any comments from the floor!"

"Then I would like permission to speak," Lily replied.

Again, Dr. Donsky looked over to Dr. Tusen-Takk, who nodded for Lily to proceed.

"As you have so clearly stated," Lily began. "We have only been in the Galápagos Island for a little over forty-eight hours. For some of you girls, the ocean is like your second home, but for some of us, the water is unfamiliar, and if we're being honest, we're afraid. Today, I operated a submarine for the first time in my life! I know that was also true for Abby-Marie and many others of us. For Isabela to be shouting orders and playing bumper cars down there today was totally unacceptable!"

"How many of you girls agree with Lily?" asked Dr. Tusen-Takk as she turned to face the girls behind her. Faith immediately raised her hand, then Natasha, then Grace, and finally Evie slowly raised her hand and joined them to condemn Isabela's behavior.

"Who would disagree with Lily's observations?" Dr. Tusen-Takk continued.

Anna Andersen quickly raised her hand, then Mikako, and then reluctantly, Ruth.

"Ruth, why are you choosing to defend Isabela?"

"Because I think there are times when we find ourselves in a crisis and it's more important to act first and consider 'the rules' second," answered Ruth. "Although, I think Isabela could be more patient," she added, just to prove she could see both sides.

"I realize you ladies have faced a life and death situation

today," responded Dr. Tusen-Takk. "And with all guilt and blame aside, I believe the most important lesson I've learned today is that we need to slow down and spend more time getting some of you girls comfortable with living on a ship and learning to swim in the ocean."

"I agree!" shouted Lily.

"As for you Isabela…" continued Dr. Tusen-Takk. "In many ways you're a hero, and in many others you're the villain of this story. I believe you should be suspended from operating an Aquadoodle for an indefinite period. You will also be required to work with Sven in the kitchen for one month. That means up at five a.m. every day to prepare breakfast."

"Isabela, do you accepted the punishment you have been given, and are you willing to comply?" asked Dr. Donsky.

"Yes," responded Isabela, her eyes filling with tears.

"Then this tribunal is adjourned," Dr. Donsky concluded.

"This tribunal may be over," said Dr. Tusen-Takk, "but this discussion has only begun. We want to encourage honest communication at the Wonderwood Academy. If you've got an opinion about what happened out there today, I want to hear it."

"Do you want to know what I think?" shouted Abby-Marie, who had returned from her cabin and was now standing at the door of the dining room next to Lady Burd.

"I think… I think I want to get off this ship and go home!" said Abby-Marie, glaring at Isabela with eyes that could kill. "Isabela, you're nothing but a bully, and because of you, I almost died out there!" Abby-Marie spat on the floor and then stomped it like a bug. "I hate you!"

13

POISON IN YOUR POCKET

It was two o'clock in the morning, and Abby-Marie couldn't sleep. She had been lying in her bed for hours, reliving every terrifying moment that happened the day before. "I wish this was a nightmare," she thought to herself. "Then at least I would be sleeping, and in the morning, I would wake up and all this would be over." She grabbed her pillow and pulled it to her face and screamed.

"Are you okay?" Lily asked from the bed just two feet away.

"I'm fine," said Abby-Marie, but she knew it was a lie. "I can't sleep," she sighed. "I think I need to go see Lady Burd."

Abby-Marie slipped out of her bed and into the hallway, trying to remember which cabin was Lady Burd's. She walked down the corridor shaking her head. Every cabin door looked the same. When she came to the end of the hallway, she looked up at the last door. There was a small paper note taped to the door.

"Abby-Marie, if you need to talk, just knock. It doesn't matter what time it is. I'm always happy to listen." The note was signed, "Your friend, Lady Burd."

Abby-Marie smiled. "How did Lady Burd know I would need her? How did she know I would come in the middle of the night?" Abby-Marie took a breath and knocked. "Abby-Marie, is that you?" Lady Burd whispered. "Just a minute. I'll be right with you."

Lady Burd put on her bathrobe and opened the door. "Let's go up to the dining hall," she said quietly, trying not to wake Dr. Tusen-Takk in the bed next to hers. Abby-Marie looked past Lady Burd and saw an image of the Wonderwood Academy's chancellor that would be hard to forget. The large Norwegian woman was sleeping with her mouth open, and a stream of drool was running down the side of her cheek. She was wearing the hockey helmet Sven had given her, and her big feet were sticking out from the bottom of the bed.

"She's had a hard week," whispered Lady Burd, quickly closing the door trying to preserve the dignity of her respected colleague.

"Shall I make us some tea?" asked Lady Burd as she switched on an electric tea kettle on the counter in the back of the dining hall. "These conditions aren't ideal for tea making," she continued, "but any port in a storm I always say. What would you think of some lavender chamomile tea?"

"Sounds perfect."

"I find it helps me sleep," said Lady Burd as she plugged in the kettle and sat down on a stool across from Abby-Marie. "How are you feeling?"

There was a knock on the door. A small mousy voice came from the doorway across the room. It was Lily.

"Pardon, may I join you?"

"I believe this needs to be private," said Lady Burd.

"No, it's okay," replied Abby-Marie. "Lily is my roommate, and I want her to hear this too."

Lady Burd pulled out another cup, placed it on the prep table, and poured boiling water over a fresh tea bag. Abby-Marie took in a long, deep breath as she prepared to tell a story she had been holding inside for an awfully long time.

"It has to do with my little brother, Theo," she sighed as the words escaped from deep inside her. "When he was four, and I was five, our family was getting ready to go on holiday. My dad rented a large yacht, and our family was going to spend a month sailing around the Greek Islands. The ship was docked, and my mom and dad were busy loading supplies and getting everything ready for our trip. Theo and I were playing together on the deck. Theo loved cars, so we pretended to be race car drivers and started running around the deck. Theo wanted to race, so we both started to run faster and faster. He was ahead of me and wouldn't let me get past, so I pushed him. I pushed him hard, and he fell. He hit his head on the deck and rolled off the side of the ship and into the water. I stood there frozen. I couldn't move. I couldn't speak. I don't know how long it was, but when my mom came back, she asked me where Theo was. I still couldn't speak. My mom must've noticed that I was looking into the water, so she ran to the side of the ship and saw Theo's body face down in the water. She screamed for my dad, and the two of them dove in and pulled his body back on deck. I remember his skin was white, and his lips were blue. He didn't move. My parents started giving him CPR. I can still see my dad screaming for someone to call an ambulance as he leaned over and gave Theo mouth-to-mouth. My mother was screaming too. It seemed like hours with me standing there paralyzed. I'm sure it was just minutes, but Theo finally came back to life. I remember his first gasp for air. It was what allowed me to move again. I dropped to my knees and started to cry. That's all I remember. I couldn't move. I was supposed to be watching out for him, but I didn't. He almost drowned because of me. That's why I hate the water."

Lady Burd and Lily's eyes filled with tears. "And you've been hiding that secret all these years?" asked Lily.

Lady Burd gently turned Abby-Marie's face to hers and looked her in the eyes. "Having hate in your heart is like carrying poison in your pocket. You walk around waiting for the right moment to pull it out so you can hurt the person who hurt you. You think you're getting revenge, but it's just the opposite. That poison you're carrying is seeping through your pocket and into your skin. It fills your whole body. It's not hurting anyone else, but it's killing you!"

"That's how I feel," said Abby-Marie as a tear ran down her cheek. "It feels like my heart has been poisoned. It feels like I'm dying inside." She looked up at Lady Burd.

"What should I do?"

"I know what worked for me," Lady Burd replied. She paused and closed her eyes. She thought about all the pain and hurt she carried around for so many years. She took a deep breath and whispered, "Forgiveness."

"Forgiveness?"

"That's right. It seems to me you must decide if there are some people out there you need to forgive. Now, I'm no psychologist, but I think the first person just might be yourself. I think it's time to empty your pockets."

14

RADIO WAVES

BEEP! BEEP! BEEP!

There's nothing worse than the sound of an alarm clock going off at five in the morning.

"Turn it off!" Evie groaned as she grabbed her pillow and wrapped it around her ears. Evie was hoping to sleep for at least two more hours. "Please, Isabela, just get up and go!"

Isabela slumped out of bed, slipped on her uniform, and pulled a baseball hat over her bedhead hair. The ship was dark and quiet. She walked down the dark corridor to the ship's kitchen and found Sven, who was already at work.

"You're late!" Sven scolded.

"I'm sorry," replied Isabela. "It won't happen again."

Sven didn't look up. He was busy wiping down the counters and getting things ready to make breakfast. The lights in the kitchen seemed extremely bright, the smell of freshly brewed coffee was in the air, and a small radio was playing '80s pop music.

"Oh, what a feeling, when we're dancing on the ceiling!" Sven sang along with the radio, his Norwegian accent becoming even more obvious as he sang. He failed to notice Lily and Abby-Marie standing at the doorway of his kitchen.

"Well, I don't know if we're ready to dance on the ceiling," interrupted Lily, but we've been up talking all night, and we decided we want to help with breakfast."

Abby-Marie stood silently in the doorway, trying not to look Isabela in the eyes.

"I thought you hated me," responded Isabela sharply.

"I do," said Abby-Marie, "but I don't want to."

"Then why don't you go back to bed and hate me somewhere else?"

"I want to thank you for saving my life," said Abby-Marie. "I just wish you would be kinder to me. It's not easy for me to be here."

"Well, it is for me," Isabela snapped. "This is my home, and I love it! You're making it hard for everyone to see how amazing this semester can be! And, yes, I did save your life. Do you think it was easy, pulling you from that submarine? And how was I supposed to know that a little bump in the back of your mini sub would send you out of control like that?"

"Why don't you just give us some time?" Lily asked. "I think you'll find that eventually we will learn to love this place as much as you do, but it's going to take some time. And for Abby-Marie, it's a little more complicated than it is for the rest of us."

"How much time?" said Isabela.

"I don't know," answered Lily. "Let's just say that we came to help this morning because we don't want it to take too long."

Sven cleared his throat. "Speaking of taking too long, do you girls think we could get going on breakfast?"

Sven grabbed two more aprons and handed them to Lily and Abby-Marie. "Do any of you girls know how to scramble eggs?"

"I do," responded Abby-Marie, who was glad to get past the awkward exchange. "I can make eggs any style… scrambled, poached, over-easy, omelets, souffles, you name it!"

"*C'est tres magnifique!*" Sven grinned, trying his best to speak a little French. "It's nice to have an experienced cook to help me in the kitchen.

"I can boil water," said Lily.

"And I can chop things up!" added Isabela.

Sven started pulling out ingredients from the large refrigerator behind him.

"Abby-Marie, you make the eggs. Lily, you can make the toast. I'll fry up the bacon, and, Isabela, you can chop up the seaweed!"

"Yuck!" protested Isabela. "Give me something else to do!"

Sven paused and looked down at his shiny new sausage grinder. "What if we made dog sausage? You know, sausage of the dog?"

"You can't do that!" said Isabela.

"Isn't that illegal?" Lily argued.

Sven looked surprised. "What's the problem? We'll
make them very small," he said, holding up his fingers
no more than an inch apart. "You know, tiny. One bite.
A treat!"

"I think he means sausages FOR dogs," Abby-Marie
explained, "not sausages made from dogs!"

"Oh, yes, never!" Sven said in embarrassment, trying
to defend himself. "I love dogs! I love your Wonder
Doodles. No, never, not sausage OF dogs, sausage
FOR dogs."

"Whew," said Lily in relief. "I thought we had a real
problem on our hands.

"Just as long as you don't try putting seaweed in those
sausages," said Isabela, "I think Galileo would love
them!"

"Okay, all clear now," said Sven. "Let's get back to work
now. We make breakfast. Scrambled eggs and bacon!"

Sven reached over to raise the volume on the radio, hoping to recover from the awkward moment and his somewhat less than perfect English. But instead of raising the volume, he changed the station on his small radio. Loud electronic noises started buzzing from the radio's tiny speakers.

"What is that?" asked Isabela.

"I don't know," answered Sven, "but take a look at that electric mixer on the counter!"

The three girls looked over at the counter and watched as the electric mixer turned on and then set itself to blend at the highest setting.

"What's happening?" asked Lily.

Sven picked up the radio and moved it to the other side of the kitchen. Suddenly, the microwave turned on and started cooking. He moved it again, and the toaster started heating up.

"Quick, turn the station!" shouted Abby-Marie. "Or better, just turn that thing off!"

Sven switched off the radio and all the appliances went dead. He turned the radio on again and they all turned on again.

"Okay, now that's weird," said Isabela.

"Oh, this is more than just weird," said Sven, turning off the radio one last time. "I think someone is up to no good!"

15

HECTOR'S ULTIMATUM

Everyone gathered in the dining hall at seven a.m. sharp. There was an uneasiness in the air as the rest of the Wonderwood Girls were curious to know if Isabela and Abby-Marie were still at war.

When the meal was over, Captain Carlos stood to his feet. "I'm happy to say that Abby-Marie's Aquadoodle has been repaired, and everything is back to working order!" he announced, trying to bring some redemption to the incident of the day before.

Abby-Marie and Lily were too tired to get excited. They

rested their heads on the table, trying hard not to fall asleep.

"Your scrambled eggs were a huge success," Lily said with a big yawn, trying to encourage her sleepy roommate.

"And your toast was amazing!" laughed Abby-Marie. "I think that was the best toast I've ever tasted!"

"Right," said Lily in disbelief. "I guess the real success story from the kitchen this morning were those tiny little sausages Sven made for the Wonder Doodles!"

"I didn't think Joey could jump so high!" said Ruth as she held out a tiny sausage treat four feet off the deck. Joey was a small, energetic border doodle that weighed less than five pounds. The little puppy focused on the meaty prize suspended above him; he crouched down and sprang into the air catching the sausage in his mouth.

"Wow, what's in those things?" asked Dr. Bouchon. "I wish I could make a healthy snack like that!"

"Well...not so healthy," started Sven. "Mostly fat and food scraps."

"Oh," responded Dr. Bouchon in disappointment. "Well, then maybe I could help with the healthy part."

Sven frowned. He didn't like the idea of anyone messing with his recipes.

"It looks like I need to go down and make another batch!" said Sven, trying to escape.

As he turned to leave, the girls looked over the side of the Seadoodle and saw an Ecuadorian coast guard ship glide in alongside. Hector the Inspector tied off his ship and climbed up the ladder and onto the deck.

"What's going on here?" he demanded as the Wonder Doodles bounced and played around his feet. "It looks like these dogs are out of control! Where is Nina? Where are your professors? This needs to stop! Now!"

Dr. Nina Cruz ran out onto the deck from the dining hall where the professors were finishing up their breakfast. "It's okay, Hector, the girls were just having a little fun with their puppies. Everything is under control!"

"Well, it doesn't look like it!" Hector's voice started to tremble.

"What's wrong?" Nina asked.

Hector was deeply troubled. "They're coming!" he said. "The United Nations. They're coming down here to check on our situation!"

"Situation?" asked Nina, a little confused. "Why don't you come inside, and we can talk about it with Carlos and the professors."

The Wonderwood Girls immediately sensed the gravity of the situation, put down their sausages, and followed Dr. Cruz and Hector back into the dining hall. Dr. Thomsen pulled out an extra chair, and Lady Burd placed a cup of coffee in front of the troubled man.

"*Gracias,*" he said, his hands still trembling.

"What is it?" asked Dr. Tusen-Takk. "How can we help?"

"Poachers," answered the inspector. "It's the only explanation I can come up with."

"Explanation for what?" asked Captain Carlos.

"All the missing animals!"

"Missing?"

"Hundreds of them. Who knows, maybe even thousands. We can't figure it out, but all over the Galápagos our numbers are decreasing. No more seals, no more birds, no more turtles!"

"We found a sea turtle yesterday," interrupted Dr. Martinez, trying to help. "It was trapped in a ball of seaweed and tangled up in a fishing net. I put a tag on it, so we should be able to track its location!"

"If it is poachers, then this could get very dangerous," added Lady Burd. "I've dealt with some of these guys before in Africa. They mean business, and if anyone starts to threaten their operation, well... I don't have to tell you what happens next."

"The United Nations got wind of it," said Hector. "They're sending down a team to evaluate our situation. You all know what that means!"

"No, we don't," said Grace. "What does that mean?"

"It means bad press. When this story gets out, the internet will be filled with stories of how Ecuador cannot protect the Galápagos Islands! These islands have been designated as a United Nations World Heritage site. It means the world is watching and the Ecuadorian government will be disgraced. It means the president is going to be publicly humiliated, and when that happens, people lose their jobs, and the first one to get fired will be me!"

"I think we should track that turtle!" said Dr. Martinez.

"Her name is Shellie!" added Faith.

"That sea turtle just might lead us to the location of those poachers!"

"Yes," said Dr. Tusen-Takk. "And it just might get us all killed!"

"What other option do we have?" asked Hector the Inspector in desperation. "The United Nations investigation team will be here in two days!"

"I say we go after these guys!" said Dr. Donsky. "Poachers need to be brought to justice!"

"I say we let the authorities take care of this!" said Lady Burd wisely.

"I am the authorities!" answered Hector in a defeated funk. "It's going to take an army to figure this out and get everything back to normal in less than forty-eight hours!"

"It just seems too risky to get involved," answered Dr. Tusen-Takk.

"Well, the Wonderwood Academy is already involved," said Hector the Inspector. "You have forty-eight hours to get these dogs under control. They need to be below deck in a clean, well-ventilated space. I expect to see the world's finest floating kennels when I return."

"And if we don't?" asked Dr. Tusen-Takk.

"If you don't?" answered Hector sharply. "If you don't, you and your students will need to start packing your bags, and I'm pretty sure I wouldn't be too far behind you."

16
RUTH'S FAN CAM

"Well then, Mr. Hector Muñoz, inspector and protector of the Galápagos Islands, you've made our mission very clear," Dr. Tusen-Takk stated with authority. "I believe we have our work cut out for us," she continued. "So… if you would be so kind as to give us the room."

"Of course," the inspector replied, realizing he was being asked to leave. "I'll be back in less than two days' time, and remember, world class kennels, WORLD CLASS!"

All ten Wonderwood Girls stood and moved forward to take part in this important meeting.

"Girls, I'm afraid I need you to leave as well," Dr. Tusen-Takk added with a frown.

"It's not fair!" Anna Andersen protested as she left the dining hall with the others.

"That's right," added Mikako. "If this is a situation of global importance and it directly affects us and the future of the Wonderwood Academy, then I think we should be a part of it!"

"Global importance?" Grace repeated after a pause. "The future of the Wonderwood Academy? Evie, don't you think we need to be filming this?"

"Of course," Evie answered, "but they're never going to let us bring a camera in there!"

Ruth smiled. "Don't worry, ladies, I've already got that covered. This morning I got up early and taped my small underwater camera to one of the blades on the ceiling fan in the dining hall."

"Is it connected to the Wi-Fi?" asked Lily.

"Of course," answered Ruth.

"Well, then what are we waiting for? We can be watching

this meeting from your room!"

The other eight girls followed the Middletree sisters downstairs, and all ten crammed into Ruth and Grace's cabin. Ruth pulled out a laptop, dialed into the camera feed, and an image of the dining hall appeared.

"The way I see it," Dr. Tusen-Takk was saying, "We must choose whether to get involved in this missing animal crisis or protect our own interests and focus our attention on setting up 'world class' kennels in less than two days."

As the professors argued, things in Ruth and Grace's cabin were getting a little cramped.

"Move over!" complained Evie from the back of Ruth's bed. "I can't see, and I'm the director! Are we recording this?"

"Of course," answered Ruth. "Now, everybody settle down. I don't want to miss any of this!"

"On the first matter," Lady Burd began. "I hold my position. We have a school to run, and it's far too dangerous to get involved with an international poaching ring."

"Besides," continued Dr. Broomfield, "imagine what the press will do to our reputation if they capture images of us harboring these 'diseased-filled dogs'!"

"I think she's right," added Dr. Matsura. "One bad story, and I lose face. My research career could be over!"

"She's right," said Dr. Yaron. "I've seen it happen before. One bad story and you're gone!"

"I disagree," interrupted Dr. Donsky. "If we let these poachers steal all the wildlife from this place, it may never be the same!"

"Let's at least try to do something!" pleaded Dr. Martinez. "I put a tracker tag on that sea turtle. Why don't we spend a minute and get its location?"

"Her name is Shellie!" Faith shouted at the computer.

"She can't hear you!" said Natasha.

"I know," said Faith, "but that turtle has a name!"

Dr. Martinez pulled up an image on the screen at the front of the dining hall.

"According to the GPS data, our turtle friend is swimming somewhere in the middle of this bay."

"Well, that doesn't give us much to go on," said Dr. Thomsen.

"Why don't we look at the turtle's movement over time?" asked Dr. Broomfield. "I'd like to see where she's been since you placed that tracker tag."

Dr. Martinez clicked a few computer keys, and a new image filled the screen.

"Wow," said Dr. Martinez a bit surprised. "It looks like this turtle is moving in a pattern. It goes back and forth between the island behind us and a specific location in the middle of the bay."

"That's odd," said Dr. Tusen-Takk.

"Yes, and she's been back and forth over twenty times," added Dr. Martinez.

"I still don't think it's something we want to get mixed up in!" repeated Lady Burd. "If you ask me, I think we should be putting all our efforts into setting up those kennels!"

"Lady Burd is right," said Dr. Broomfield. "No kennels, no Wonderwood Academy!"

"Sure," said Dr. Maggie Middletree, "but where are we going to put them? It is stuffy and cramped below deck."

"Captain Carlos showed me a storage room below deck that could work," replied Dr. Thomsen. "My main concern with that space is air flow."

"Why don't we install some ceiling fans?" offered Dr. Mitch Middletree as he walked over to the wall and switched on the fan above them.

"No, Dad! Don't!" screamed Ruth from the cabin below.

The image on her computer screen started to blur as her camera started spinning in circles.

"I can't watch this!" said Grace, "It's making me dizzy!"

"This footage will be unusable!" said Evie.

Dr. Donsky got up from her seat and stood under the fan to feel the power it produced. "Fans like this could work," she said, "but we're going to need a lot of them!"

Sven poked his head through the doorway of the dining hall.

"Sorry to interrupt your meeting," said Sven, who was holding his radio and an electric toothbrush. "I have something I think you should see."

"What's that?" asked Abby-Marie, trying to make sense of the swirling image on the screen.

"You mean who is that?" said Lily, trying to figure it out too. "I think it's Sven, and he's showing them the radio!"

"We need this footage!" said Isabela. "I think he's trying

to show them what those radio frequencies were doing back in the kitchen!"

When Sven switched on the radio, the electric toothbrush in his hand started to buzz. He changed the radio station, and the toothbrush turned off.

"We discovered something strange this morning," Sven explained. "These radio frequencies affect electronic devices. Take a look!"

Sven changed the station, and the ceiling fan above them slowed down and came to a stop.

"Yes! Thank you!" shouted Evie. "We need to get this for the documentary!"

Sven changed the station a few more times, and the coffeemaker started brewing. Then the tea kettle began to boil.

"What could be causing that?" asked Dr. Buchon.

"I don't know, but you can bet I'm going to get to the bottom of this," replied Dr. Maggie Middletree.

Sven switched the station one last time, and the ceiling fan turned back on. As the blades started to spin again, Ruth's small underwater camera came loose and dropped to the floor at Sven's feet.

Sven picked up the camera. "I think this is one more thing we need to get to the bottom of!"

17
THE PELICAN

Sven took a closer look at the small camera that landed at his feet and pulled off the sticky tape that was holding it to the ceiling fan.

"It looks like there are someone's initials on the back," said Sven. "Hmmm, R.M. Does anyone know what R.M. stands for?"

"I have a hunch," answered Dr. Mitch. "I have a daughter with those initials."

"Oh hi, Dad. You found my camera!" Ruth was standing just outside the dining hall with a larger camera on her shoulder. Evie, Grace, and Natasha were standing beside her.

"We're here to do some interviews for the documentary film you asked us to produce!" Grace added, trying to cover the fact they were guilty of spying on the professors' meeting.

"What was a camera doing up on the blade of that ceiling fan?" Mitch said sternly to his two daughters.

"We didn't mean to be spying on you guys," contested Evie. "It just happened!"

"Yeah, Dad," said Ruth. "I put that camera up there so we could get some great video shots of our mealtimes and class sessions!"

"Well, don't you think we deserve some privacy?" asked Mitch. "Professors need a place where they can be vulnerable and debate ideas without their students poking in. Anyway, what did you film? Was the footage any good?"

"It looks great!" said Evie, "except for the part when you started the fan spinning. I think that video is unusable, but the rest is amazing. I mean a group of twelve professors who are worried, anxious, and just a bit terrified fighting over whether they should be a part of rescuing one of the world's greatest collections of wildlife. Well... that's what makes a great documentary film!"

"Maybe so," said Dr. Mitch, "but I think people have the right to know they're being filmed."

"From now on, we'll let people know," said Natasha. "Do you think we could get a few interviews right now?" she added, trying to change the subject and move past the controversy. "Hey, guys, let's get an interview with Sven demonstrating how the radio turns on his toothbrush!"

Sven was standing a few feet away, demonstrating for Dr. Maggie and Dr. Matsura how radio frequencies controlled his electronic devices.

"Sven, could we get a demonstration for our film?" asked Grace as she motioned for Ruth to begin recording. "Now, please, tell us what you've discovered."

Sven switched on the radio and held up his toothbrush. "Well, it appears there are some strange radio frequencies being transmitted in this area. From what your professors tell me, the frequencies are very powerful, so powerful they are bleeding into radio frequencies and other remote-controlled devices. Right now, it's still a mystery where they are coming from and who is producing them."

"Thank you," said Grace in response. "And, Mom, what's your take on this strange phenomenon. Foul play?"

"Oh dear," answered Dr. Maggie. "I'm sorry, honey, but I don't have time to speculate. Please give me some time to run this through our spectrum analyzer. I'll have more scientific data in a few hours. It's just not scientific to speculate."

"Let's interview Dr. Martinez next," said Evie. "I want to learn more about how they're tracking our sea turtle friend, Shellie!"

Dr. Martinez agreed to do the interview and showed the girls how her computer was able to track the sea turtle's position in the water.

"It looks like she's got a regular bus route!" said Dr. Martinez for the camera. "Take a look at her activity over the past eighteen hours. She's making a loop back and forth between the island and this location in the middle of the bay."

"But there's nothing there!" said Ruth. "Why would a turtle swim all that way for nothing?"

"That's what we're trying to figure out," answered Dr. Martinez. "It's what I do. I try to figure out the behavior of animals."

"Then can you figure out the behavior of Isabela and Abby-Marie?" asked Natasha. "They seem to have it out for one another."

"I just work with animals in the wild," smiled Dr. Martinez.

"Well, it's getting pretty awkward between the two of them," said Evie.

"Hey, would you mind if we took one of your tracking tags?" asked Grace. "I'd like to get a couple of close-ups for the documentary."

"Sure," said Dr. Martinez. "Just make sure I get it back. These things aren't cheap."

"Okay, girls," said Evie to her film crew. "I think that's enough for now, let's get back to my cabin and do some editing! I want to see the footage we recorded from the cciling fan."

Back in Evie's room, the girls set up a laptop computer and started uploading all the footage they had recorded.

"Play back the part where Sven turned on his toothbrush with the radio," said Grace.

Ruth loaded the video clip and hit play. The frequency played on the screen and over the speakers.

"Whoa, that's a bit loud, don't you think?" said Evie.

"Sorry," apologized Natasha.

"Play it back again."

Again, Ruth played the clip just as a large pelican landed on the window frame that surrounded the porthole above their heads. As if on cue, the bird tapped the window three times.

"What? Play that part again!" said Evie.

Ruth hit the play button, and again the bird tapped on the glass three times.

"That sound is controlling that bird!" shouted Natasha.

"Quick," said Grace. "We need to get this tracker tag on that bird!"

18

THE SECRET MEETING

Grace and Natasha rushed out onto the deck as Ruth and Evie played the video clip over and over from the cabin below. The strange bird tapped the window three times whenever it heard the recording.

"It's as if the bird has no choice," said Natasha. "It has to obey!"

"Let's get this tag around its ankle," answered Grace as she quietly reached out and grabbed it from behind. "Gotcha!"

"Quick, tag it and set it free!" Natasha said as she signaled for Ruth and Evie to stop playing the clip.

Grace clipped on the tracker tag and turned to release the bird, when Dr. Broomfield caught the suspicious pair in the act.

"What are the two of you doing with that bird?" she asked.

"I think it got lost," said Natasha.

"We're trying to help it find its way home," added Grace as she lifted the bird toward the sky and launched it into the air.

"Well, we need you guys downstairs to help with the kennels," ordered Dr. Broomfield. "Dr. Tusen-Takk said the kennels come first! I don't know if you girls realize what's at stake here. No kennels, no school! After that, and only after that, we just might have time to help lost birds!"

Ruth, Grace, Evie, and Natasha knew that what they just witnessed was no accident. Someone or something was transmitting audio frequencies that could control the behavior of wild animals, and it must have had something to do with all the missing animals in the Galápagos Islands.

"We've got to do something," said Ruth.

Grace quickly spread the word to the other six Wonderwood Girls. They decided to have their own private meeting on the ship's deck after dark.

"I don't like the feeling of this," said Faith. "Don't you think we should let Dr. Tusen-Takk and the professors know what we're doing?"

"We can't," answered Evie. "It's too risky."

"That's right," added Ruth. "The professors are worried the press will report that they are the ones responsible for the all the disappearing wildlife. If that leaks out, their careers could be ruined!"

"And then, we can all say goodbye to the Wonderwood Academy!" added Lily for good measure.

"I agree," said Anna, raising her voice above the others. "It's up to us to save the Wonderwood Academy! We need to start tonight!"

"Shhhhh," Grace cautioned, not wanting to be overheard.

"I agree with Anna. I've been tracking a bird we found tapping at our window earlier this afternoon, and it's doing the same thing as Shellie, the sea turtle. It flies to the island and then flies out to the middle of the bay. It's been doing that ever since I set it free five hours ago."

"Okay then," said Ruth. "Who's up for a midnight submarine expedition to the island?"

"Not me!" said Abby-Marie.

"I can't go either," said Isabela. "I've been grounded until further notice."

"That's okay," said Evie. "Isabela, Abby-Marie, and Lily can all stay here. They have to get up earlier and make breakfast anyway.

"And what about the Wonder Doodles?" asked Natasha. "Are they coming too?"

"Of course!" said Ruth. "We need them for back up. They can sense trouble a mile away!"

"But won't they start barking and wake everyone up?" worried Grace.

"I've got that covered," answered Abby-Marie. "I'll just make another batch of Sven's amazing mini sausages. If the doodles start acting up, just slip them one of these!" she said, holding up one of Sven's little sausage treats.

"Okay then, it's settled," said Anna. "We all meet on the rear deck with our Wonder Doodles at the stroke of midnight. Then we will head to the island under the cover of darkness."

"And……," started Evie.

"And what?" asked Faith, still nervous about the whole thing.

"And… I say we bring the camera! Don't you all think this would be an amazing scene to add to our documentary? Imagine! Submarines in the middle of the night underwater in the dark! We land at the beach and begin searching for clues!"

"I'm in!" said Ruth, eager to capture every minute with her camera.

"And I think we should all carry one of these," said Grace, holding up a handful of the tracker tags she borrowed from Dr. Martinez's research supplies.

"That's a great idea," said Isabela. "Then if anything goes wrong, we'll know exactly where to find you.

"Do I staple it to my ear?" asked Anna, not quite sure what to do with an animal tracking tag.

"No, just put it in your pocket," answered Grace.

"Are you sure we shouldn't at least let Lady Burd know what we're doing?" asked Faith one more time.

"No!" said Ruth. "We'll let them know when we have concrete evidence to share. Until then, it's better for us to keep this all between us. If we do our job, we'll be back in our beds long before breakfast, and I'll have some amazing footage to add to our documentary film!"

"Great!" said Grace. "Then it's agreed. We meet at midnight!"

Once again, a pelican perched high above the deck turned as the camera embedded on the top of its head zoomed in on the circle of girls sitting below.

Back at Colossus Control, deep underground, two men watched the Wonderwood Girls making their plan.

"Those pesky girls are starting to meddle with my operation," said The Dentist. "They're planning to go to the island tonight!"

"What are you going to do about it?" asked the second man.

"I think we need to take action, fast!" said The Dentist. "Boss, do I have permission to move from Project Tooth Implantation to Project Extinction?"

The man standing behind him didn't hesitate. "Permission granted."

19

MIDNIGHT MISSION

It was just a few minutes past midnight, and the Wonderwood Girls were standing on the rear deck, each holding on to the collar of their Wonder Doodle trying to keep their dogs quiet.

"I think it will go faster if you guys get into your mini subs now," suggested Isabela. "The doodles won't like it, but at least then no one will hear them if they start barking. Once you get in, I'll lower you down to the water as fast as I can."

"These will help," said Abby-Marie as she held up a large bucket of Sven's mini sausages. "Everyone, take a handful. I'm sure they'll come in handy!"

"Let's roll!" said Ruth as she climbed into the cockpit of her submarine with her little border doodle, Joey, in her arms.

"Easy for you," whispered Anna as she tried to coax her 40-pound Huskydoodle into her sub with a sausage.

"Everyone, wait for me once you get under water," ordered Ruth. "We'll go over our plan once we're all out there together."

"Does everyone have their tracker tag?" asked Grace making sure to double check.

Ruth was the last one to get into her mini sub. Just before she closed the hatch of her cockpit, she handed Isabela her camera. "I want to say something before we leave," she said pointing to the red button and motioning for Isabela to start filming.

"Some might criticize us for taking on this mission," she said to the camera, sounding like they were about to make history. "But we believe we are seeking the best interests of our professors and the Wonderwood Academy. This is Ruth Middletree, and as we plunge into the murky depths, we hope that what we do tonight will forever benefit the Galápagos Islands and the animals who live here. Godspeed!"

Isabela handed back her camera. Ruth closed the hatch and Isabela lowered her submarine down to the water below. Isabela, Abby-Marie, and Lily watched as she submerged her Aquadoodle and drove forward to join the rest of the team.

"We'll have breakfast waiting for you when you return!" said Isabela waving goodbye. She turned to look at Abby-Marie and Lily. "I hope we're doing the right thing."

"Me too," said Lily. "C'mon, there's not much we can do now. Let's try to get some sleep."

In just a few seconds, Ruth's submarine passed the others as she took the lead. Seven small submarines moved forward in single file. There was a silvery reflection of the moon on the surface of the water above them, all around there were tiny little bioluminescent creatures floating in the water like fireflies.

"It's beautiful!" said Mikako. "I've never seen anything like this!"

"Yikes!" screamed Natasha as a school of sharp-toothed barracuda swam past. "Me neither."

"Okay, everyone, this is our mission," said Ruth. "Our

goal is to land on the island and do some reconnaissance."

"Reconna- what?" said Faith.

"Reconnaissance. That means we're going to explore the island and report what we find. We're also going to do some filming, so everyone follow me single file. Anna, I need you to bring up the rear. Make sure no one gets lost, and no one gets left behind. You've got our backs!"

"Aye, aye, captain," Anna responded as she maneuvered her sub to the end of the line. "Everyone, I've got your backs!"

"The air in here smells like sausage, seaweed, dog breath," complained Evie.

"Mine too," said Natasha, "but I guess it's better than DaVinci barking in my ear all night!"

"Let's keep the intercom clear," ordered Ruth. "We're coming up to the underwater seaweed farm, and I want to make sure no one gets tangled up."

Ruth shifted course and increased the distance between her sub and the long strands of seaweed to her left.

"What's that?" asked Grace, a bit startled. "Is that Shellie?"

A large sea turtle poked its head out from the rows of the floating green plants.

"It can't be," said Mikako. "It doesn't have a tracker tag."

"But it does have something else," answered Grace. "What's that on its back? It looks like a basket."

Evie changed her direction to get a closer look at the turtle, who seemed unaffected by all the attention. The basket on its back was filled with seaweed.

"Look, there's another one!" said Faith. "And another!"

Nine sea turtles with baskets on their backs followed each other in a line.

"They're harvesting!" shouted Anna. "They're harvesting our seaweed!"

"And it looks like they're heading to the island," added Grace.

"I say we follow them," said Ruth, who was trying to film the turtles and drive her submarine at the same time. "I think they'll take us to whatever it is that's making them do this."

The nine sea turtles and seven mini subs arrived at the beach ten minutes later. The girls maneuvered their Aquadoodles, so the bottom halves of their subs were wedged in the soft sand below and the glass cockpits were sticking out of the water. The girls opened their hatches, and warm island air filled their lungs.

"Ahhh, fresh air!" Evie cheered.

"Okay, let's keep quiet," ordered Ruth, stepping out into the water and onto the beach. "We need to follow these turtles and find out what they're doing with all that seaweed."

"I'm staying here!" answered Faith. "I'm not so sure this is something we should be doing! Didn't Hector say that all dogs were supposed to stay off the islands?"

"I think it's more important to find out what's happening with all these missing animals!" countered Anna. "Besides, I think Ruth said, 'No one gets lost, and no one gets left behind.'"

A large sea lion with a basket on its back bumped into Faith's submarine, almost causing it to fall on its side.

Faith's large Saint Berdoodle, Copernicus, nudged her on the shoulder with his big nose. "I don't like the looks of this, Copernicus," whispered Faith. "It feels like a trap!"

20
ON THE ISLAND

"Quiet, everybody!" Evie ordered as Ruth switched on her camera and began to film. "I want a shot of us walking onto the island for the first time."

"Oh, this keeps getting worse," moaned Faith as she watched the rest of her group march onto the beach. "Now we're actually recording evidence that will send us all to jail!"

"Come on, Faith!" Anna whispered. "We're only going to be here for fifteen minutes. It will be over in no time, and then we can all go back to bed!"

"You know what?" said Faith. "I don't care if it takes fifteen seconds. I'm not going!" She grabbed Copernicus by the collar. "I'll see you guys when you get back!"

"You're going to regret it!" shouted Anna, turning back to catch up with the rest of the group. "It's our fifteen minutes of fame!"

Faith reached up and pulled the glass hatch over her head and then reversed her mini sub back underwater. "It's okay, you guys go get famous," she muttered under her breath. "Me and Copernicus are going to wait in our submarine."

The rest of the girls started weaving their way up the path and into the dense jungle that surrounded the beach.

"Just follow these animals. And, Ruth, you keep filming!" said Evie. "That's where we're going to find our story!"

The path they followed was wide and well-worn from the countless animals who traveled back and forth. The trail was bordered by the dense brush of a tropical jungle. The mosquitos were unbearable.

"Ouch," screamed Grace, slapping the side of her neck. "These mosquitos are killing me!"

"Hang in there, Grace!" said Ruth and pointed, "Look!"

The path ahead of them opened to a large clearing that was the size of two or three football fields. The girls could not believe what they saw by the light of the moon.

"It looks like Noah's ark!" said Evie.

"Have you ever seen so many animals?" Mikako gasped with astonishment. "There are thousands of them!"

In the large clearing, the girls saw hundreds and hundreds of shipping containers the size of school buses. Walking back and forth in straight lines were turtles, birds, sea lions, penguins, and monkeys. They all walked, flew, and waddled like robots on a mission. Each one had a job to do, and it appeared they had no choice but to do it.

"They looked like they've been programmed!" said Ruth.

"Just like that bird tapping at our window," added Evie.

"This is weird," said Grace. "I don't think we should be here!"

"I think you're right!" said a voice from behind them.

They all turned around to see an enormous Galápagos

turtle with an oversized camera on its head. "You shouldn't have come here!"

"Who are you?" shouted Ruth looking straight into the lens of the camera. "What's going on here? This is illegal!"

"Well, well, those are some pretty strong accusations, little girl," the voice answered. "Let's just say I'm your friendly neighborhood Dentist, and I'm part of a program to help feed the world!"

"Colossus?" Anna asked boldly.

"Oh, you girls are so much smarter than you look," answered the voice. "Yes, I work for Colossus, and you girls have stumbled upon one of our largest operations in the world. Unfortunately for you, it is supposed to be a secret!"

"You're stealing wild animals!" Natasha protested.

"Not stealing," said The Dentist. "Let's just say we're maximizing their potential."

"You've turned them into slaves, so you can make your worthless food products!" said Evie.

"You girls are really starting to annoy me," The Dentist

said, raising his voice. "I think you're slowing down our productivity!"

As The Dentist finished speaking, he pushed a button, and several large sea lions moved in to surround the girls and their dogs.

"I've been watching you for some time now, and I think it's time for you all to go! But first, I think it would be wonderful to add a few more workers to my team!"

The large sea lions grabbed the Wonder Doodles by their collars and dragged them a few yards away. The dogs tried to resist, but the sea lions were twice their size. The dogs barked back at the girls for help, but even more sea lions closed in.

"Where are you taking them?" screamed Grace.

"Let's just say they're going to make a trip to see The Dentist," said the voice with a creepy laugh.

Several birds swooped in and started circling the dogs below. Each bird had a small tank on its back, and with the push of another button, a thick, misty gas started flowing down on the Wonder Doodles.

"You're killing our puppies!" shouted Natsha.

"Oh please!" answered The Dentist. "What would I do with a pile of dead puppies? Let's just say I'm giving them a little something to help them relax."

After only a minute, the nitrous oxide gas started to take effect. The dogs stopped barking and started to fall asleep.

"Wake up, my little puppy friends!" said the voice. "It's time to take a little swim!"

The Dentist pushed another button, and six large sea lions grabbed the collar of each dog and dragged them back to the beach and into the water.

"And now for you girls!" said The Dentist with delight.

"Are you going to gas us too?" said Evie.

"Oh, I could," the voice laughed, "but I think you wouldn't prove to be very good workers. For you I have something much more interesting planned."

"Why don't you just let us go?" said Ruth as she secretly dropped two mini sausages on the ground beside her feet.

"Now that wouldn't be very interesting," said The Dentist. "Where's the fun in that? No, for you girls I have an all-expenses paid trip to Bolivia!"

The man pushed another button, and the sea lions started pushing the girls toward one of the large shipping containers filled with seaweed. As they shuffled ahead, Grace saw what Ruth was doing and she started dropping a trail of sausages too.

"Make yourselves comfortable," said the voice when they arrived at the large steel doors of the container. "You should be in Bolivia in just a few short days. Feel free to eat as much seaweed as you like!"

The girls were pushed into the container as two of the sea lions closed the large metal doors behind them. The Dentist flicked a final switch, and a third sea lion secured the latch with its nose.

"Have a great trip!" laughed The Dentist.

21
THE LONGEST NIGHT

Just off the beach, ten feet below the surface, Faith sat in her submarine trying to relax, but she couldn't. She stared at her watch as fifteen minutes turned to thirty.

"Where could they be?" she asked Copernicus, who sat patiently behind her. "I thought Anna said they would only be gone for fifteen minutes! Now I'm running out of air, and my battery is getting low!"

Faith lifted the steering wheel and returned to the surface. As the cockpit broke the water, Copernicus started to bark.

"What's going on, boy?" asked Faith. "What's out there?"

Faith looked out into the darkness and couldn't believe what she saw. Six Wonder Doodles were being led by a pack of sea lions. She called to them by name.

"Joey, DaVinci, Gutenburg! Where are you going? Stop!"

The dogs didn't respond. Copernicus barked as loudly as he could to his friends.

"It's no use," said Faith. "They look like they've been drugged!"

Back on the Seadoodle, Abby-Marie, Lily, and Isabela were doing their best to get some sleep with their Wonder Doodles on the deck.

"If this mission goes well, the girls should be back in less than an hour," said Isabela.

"Well, I won't be able to sleep until I know that they are back safe," answered Lily.

Abby-Marie pulled a blanket tight around her shoulders. Her little puppy, Edison, was resting on her lap. "Come, girls, let's make this quick. You get back here, and I'll make you the best breakfast of your life!"

But the girls on the island were nowhere close to returning to the Seadoodle. They spent the first thirty minutes shouting and pounding on the walls of the shipping container that was now their prison.

"It's no use," said Natasha, sitting down on a large mound of seaweed. "This thing is made of solid steel!"

"And I can't see a thing!" added Evie, holding her hand in front of her face. "How are we supposed to find a way out if this thing if there's no light!"

Grace sat down next to Natasha, and the two girls started to cry.

"Now don't start with the waterworks!" said Ruth. "We need to stay strong. There's a way out of here. I know it!"

"Do you think Faith will come to get us?" asked Evie.

"I don't know," answered Anna. "She seemed pretty scared when I left her back on the beach."

"Someone needs to get us out of here," cried Natasha.

"It stinks in here! And...I don't want to go to Bolivia!"

After two hours, Faith knew the mission had gone terribly wrong.

"We have to do something," she said to Copernicus, "but I'm afraid to go out there in the dark!"

She pressed a button and raised the glass hatch of her submarine. She peered out into the darkness, wishing the sun would rise.

"I don't know, Copernicus, it just seems better to stay here and wait."

Copernicus barked, not in agreement but as a warning. Out of the darkness a sea lion emerged and confronted the small submarine.

"What do you want?" Faith shouted.

A second sea lion took its place beside the first, and then a third. Faith was terrified, and Copernicus could sense her fear. He stood up in the submarine and started to growl.

"Quiet, boy!" said Faith. "We don't want to get these

guys upset!"

Copernicus didn't listen. He jumped from the submarine to try to protect Faith.

"No, stop!" shouted Faith. But it was too late. A large seagull swooped down and discharged a small cloud of gas. Copernicus tried to attack the sea lions, but his legs buckled, and he fell into the warm sand.

"Copernicus!" cried Faith.

One of the sea lions grabbed Copernicus's collar in its mouth and dragged him into the water. In less than a minute, Faith was all alone.

"How long do we wait?" asked Lily nervously.

"Why do we always assume that something has gone wrong?" said Isabela. "What if they've made an amazing discovery, and they're just waiting for the sun to rise so they can film what they've found?"

"Because that wasn't the plan!" answered Abby-Marie. "The plan was to get in and get out in less than an hour tops!"

"I say we check their tracker tags!" said Lily. "At least we'd know if they were on their way back."

The girls hurried to find Dr. Martinez's computer.

"Here it is," said Abby-Marie as she powered it up.

"It doesn't look like they've moved for hours," said Lily, pointing to a group of tracking dots on the screen. "But wait, there's one over here on the beach!"

"One of them must have stayed behind," said Abby-Marie.

"Well, I don't like the looks of this," said Lily. "They shouldn't be staying in the same place for hours!"

"I agree," said Abby-Marie. "I think it may be time to tell the professors."

"No!" protested Isabela. "My parents will kill me!"

"I don't think this is about you anymore," said Abby-Marie. "Our classmates are out there, and they need our help!"

"That's right," answered Isabela. "They need OUR help, so don't you think it would be better if we didn't get the professors involved? Look, if we leave now, we can still get back here before breakfast at seven a.m. No one would ever know!"

"I think we should at least tell Sven," Lily said. "He can cover for us until we get back."

The three girls made their way to the ship's kitchen and found Sven already busy preparing the morning meal.

"Wow, you're up early," said Abby-Marie.

"I couldn't sleep," said Sven. "All these radio frequencies flying around in the air. I don't like it."

"Here's something else you're not going to like," said Isabela. "Some of the Wonderwood Girls went to explore the island last night. They were supposed to be back four hours ago. We think they're trapped on the island."

"What?!?" Sven responded with shock. "We need to tell my cousin. We need to put a rescue team together!"

"Now wait," said Isabela. "Let's not get crazy here. We were thinking the three of us could go to the island and bring them back. You could stay here and get breakfast ready. That way, when we return, no one will know what happened."

"I don't know," said Sven. "I think…"

"Please, Sven!" pleaded Isabela. "Look, if we're not here before breakfast, you can tell Dr. Tusen-Takk and the others."

Sven reluctantly agreed. "Be back before breakfast!" he ordered.

"We will!" said Isabela. "Come on girls, let's go get our friends!"

22

COLOSSUS SPEAKS

Sven tried not to worry. It was all he could do to focus on the strawberries he was slicing for yogurt parfaits. He turned off his radio and worked in silence hoping to hear the girls' footsteps running down the hall to let him know everyone had returned safe and sound.

"Come on Wonderwood Girls," he whispered to himself. "Show me some of that WONDER!"

But the girls never came. He placed the breakfast on large trays, hoping they would arrive just in time to help him bring the meal upstairs to the dining hall. He knew all the professors would already be seated and waiting for breakfast to be served.

"Sorry, girls, but time is up. I must tell the professors what's going on and why you're not here!"

Sven left the trays on the counter and marched into the dining hall.

"Professors," he started. "I'm afraid I have some bad news..."

Sven looked around, but the dining hall was empty. The coffeemaker was cold, and the chairs hadn't been moved.

"Where is everybody?" he said out loud as he made his way to Dr. Tusen-Takk's cabin.

"Inge, Lady Burd, are you in there?"

There was no answer.

There was no answer because Dr. Tusen-Takk, Lady Burd, Captain Carlos, Nina, and all the professors were gathered up in the ship's bridge for an urgent meeting.

"I think I've figured out what's happening with these strange radio frequencies," said Dr. Maggie as she played the mysterious sounds again for everyone to hear. "These are the frequencies people use to operate remote-controlled cars, airplanes, and drones. That part was easy to figure out. The bigger question is WHY?"

"I think I might have an answer for you, Dr. Middletree," came a reply from one of the many computer monitors used to operate the ship. "Allow me to introduce myself. I am The Dentist — the one responsible for all the noise. You see, I can control almost anything and anyone with my remote-control frequencies. Take these doors for example." The Dentist looked down and pressed a button that immediately locked the two doors on either side of the bridge. Captain Carlos and Lady Burd lunged to grab the door latch, but the large metal doors were already locked tight.

"Oh, don't try to escape," said The Dentist from the computer screen in front of them. "That will only make things worse."

"Who are you?" demanded Dr. Tusen-Takk.

"I've already told you. I'm The Dentist."

"I don't want your name. I want to know who you're working for!"

"Oh, well that's an entirely different question, isn't it?" smirked The Dentist.

"Why don't you take off that mask so we can see who you are?" demanded Lady Burd.

"So many questions," answered The Dentist. "First, my mission is to take over the world by controlling its food supply, and second, if I take off this mask you would be able to recognize me and that could be detrimental to my mission."

"Are you working for Colossus?" asked Dr. Yaron.

"Wow, this really is a smart bunch," said The Dentist sarcastically. "How did you know?"

"Let's just say we had the unfortunate displeasure of doing business with your company last week," Dr. Yaron answered.

"Well, then you must already be aware of our global mission—to control the world's food supply. It's that simple."

"Where are you?" demanded Dr. Broomfield glaring at the screen.

"Ah, and yet another intriguing question from one of your distinguished professors. Let's just say I work remotely. And while we're on the topic, there's seems to be a small group of girls who decided to work remotely last night. Care to see them in action?"

The Dentist pushed another button and played a video clip he recorded of the girls being captured earlier the night before.

"Those are my daughters!" shouted Dr. Mitch. "Where are they? What have you done with our girls?"

"Oh, they're all safe and sound," said The Dentist, "but they never should have gone to my island. Now they've forced me to take drastic measures!"

"Let me see my daughters!" demanded Dr. Maggie.

"I'm afraid they're in a place where I've neglected to install any cameras," answered The Dentist, "But rest easy, Momma Bear, all your girls are safe and sound. They're locked up tight and resting on a bed of seaweed getting ready to take a lovely cruise to Bolivia!"

"Set them free at once!" said Dr. Tusen-Takk. "Set us free as well!"

"I'm afraid the time for freedom has passed," answered The Dentist. "And now, you've given me no choice but to send you off on a short cruise of your own."

As he finished, another seagull flew to one of the

windows outside the bridge and tapped on the glass three times. The Dentist pushed two more buttons. The first opened one of the small porthole windows, allowing the bird to fly into the bridge. The second released the gas from a small tank attached to its back.

"Here's a little something to put you at ease," said The Dentist. "Some call it laughing gas. I believe the technical term is nitrous oxide, but whatever it is, it seems to make animals and people a lot easier to deal with."

The Dentist pushed another button, and a white gas filled the room. The professors tried to cover their faces, but the fumes quickly overtook them and they all slumped to the floor. The Dentist flicked a few switches and turned on the ship's motor.

"Let's set a course back to the mainland," he said. "I'm afraid this bay isn't big enough to share with the Wonderwood Academy!"

Sven arrived outside the door of the bridge and watched the room fill with smoke. He tried to force the door open, but all he could do was watch as the professors collapsed to the ground.

"Sven!" Dr. Tusen-Takk struggled to speak as her hockey helmet hit the floor. "Sven, help!"

"Inge!" he shouted. "Inge!" he pounded as hard as he could on the metal door. It didn't move.

"This is bad," he said to himself. "This is really bad!"

23

FAITH IS ALL YOU NEED

Faith watched the sunrise from the safety of her submarine. Her eyes were filled with tears and her body trembled as she waited to be rescued.

"Relax, Faith," she whispered to herself. "They're coming to get you. Relax, you'll be rescued soon."

She repeated those words to herself for hours, but no one came. Then, as the sun formed the first shadow of the new day, a thought occurred to her. A thought that was quite profound for an eight-year-old girl.

"What if I'm not the one to be rescued?" she thought. "What if I'M THE RESCUER?" She choked as the words came out of her mouth. Something inside of her knew that was exactly what she should do, but Faith proceeded to have a thirty-minute argument with herself.

"Are you crazy?" she thought. "Didn't you see what happened to your dog? Copernicus was gassed and then dragged into the water by sea lions! You don't have a chance!"

"Sure," she countered, "that was bad what happened to Copernicus, but those sea lions are gone now, and if they come back, I'm sure you can outrun them."

"No, you can't!" she argued back to herself. "Sea lions can run up to fifteen miles an hour! You won't get ten feet before one of them bites you in the leg and drags you out to sea!"

"Be brave!" she told herself. "It's light out now, and you can clearly see there are no sea lions in the vicinity! You can easily hide if you can make it to the jungle. You just need to get off this beach!"

"But what about the seagulls with the gas tanks? They'll swoop in and drop that gas on you. You'll being knocked out in just a few seconds, and then what good will it do to you or your friends?"

"Come on, Faith! There's a scuba tank right behind you. Put the mask on and breathe the air in the tank. Problem solved!"

Faith went back and forth inside her head, coming up with every argument she could imagine for why she shouldn't take the risk, but in the end, she knew she had to do what was right. She knew she had to at least try to rescue her friends.

"Well, here it goes," she said as she strapped the scuba tank on her back and placed the mask over her face. She jumped out of her submarine and started running for the thick jungle cover.

"Ouch!" she shouted as she fell to the ground in the brush. "Mosquitoes! One more reason this is a terrible idea!" She slapped her leg as dozens of insects landed all over her body.

"Got to keep moving!" she said, trying to encourage herself. She scrambled through the trees and thick vegetation trying hard not to fall. "Got to stay off the path too!" she said as she struggled to pull more air from the tank. She was breathing heavily, her mask started to fog, and hundreds of mosquitoes were having a feast all over her body.

"Please let this be over!" she cried and fell to the ground. She lifted her head and pulled back a large banana leaf. The thick jungle opened to the same enormous clearing her friends encountered several hours before. She saw the animals with baskets on their backs, and the hundreds of shipping containers they were filling with oversized mangos, avocadoes, and seaweed.

"Where could they be?" she thought, scanning the area for her friends. The situation seemed hopeless. There was no way to get past all these animals undetected, and it would take days to open every shipping container and check inside.

"Think!" she told herself. "Clues! There must be some clues."

Faith took off her diving mask and squinted her eyes, looking for details. She was tempted to give up and go back to the safety of her submarine. "Keep looking!" she said. "There has to be some clue!"

Sure enough, she looked to her left and saw the path the girls had taken into the clearing. In the sandy soil there was a circle formed by the footprints of the six girls.

"Hey, what's that?" said Faith to herself.

It was a trail of tiny little sausages! Faith was tempted to leave the cover of the jungle and run in the direction of the sausages her friends had left for her to find, but she caught herself.

"Wait! I need a disguise! But what?"

Faith looked around and grabbed a large banana leaf and placed it over her back. "I'm sure I don't look much like a turtle," she thought, but it was the best she could do. She slipped her mask back over her face, took a deep breath from her scuba tank, and crawled like a turtle in the direction of those tiny sausages.

"Try to look like a turtle," she told herself, trying not to get caught. She knew she could move faster if she just stood up and ran but decided it would be better to crawl at the same speed as all the other animals all around her.

"That's it, slow and steady wins the race," she kept telling herself, but her knees were starting to bleed. "Keep moving, Faith. You can do this!" The mosquitoes continued to bite, her mask continued to fog, her shirt was soaked with sweat, and her eyes were filled with tears. She looked up, and the nearest shipping container was still twenty yards away.

"I can't do this!" she cried. She stood up and ran as fast as she could to the closest shipping container. When she arrived, she tripped, and her scuba tank banged against the metal wall of the container.

"Let us out!" came a voice from inside the container. "You'll never get away with this!"

"Ruth?" Faith couldn't believe it. "Ruth, is that you?"

24
THE ESCAPE

"Faith! Quick!" shouted Ruth through the thick metal wall of the container. "Go around the front and let us out!"

Faith pulled off her scuba tank and started looking for the container door. It took two hands to lift the latch and pry it open. The sun poured in, revealing the six, seaweed-stained prisoners inside.

"Thank you! Thank you!" her friends shouted as they rushed out into the blinding light.

"Wow, what's that awful smell?" asked Faith.

"Seaweed!" Natasha growled. "Can you believe it? That dentist dude was going to keep us locked up in there for days and send us to Bolivia!"

Ruth looked around. She knew the birds could come back, and then they would get captured all over again.

"Girls, we have to get out of here fast!"

"They took Copernicus!" said Faith. "We have to save him too!"

"I think we should go back to the Seadoodle and ask the professors for help!" said Grace.

"There's not enough time!" said Ruth. "If that evil dentist man programs our doodles, we may never see them again!"

Faith grabbed her banana leaf and pulled it over her back. "Stay off the path and follow me!" she said as she ran back into the mosquito infested jungle. "They won't find us if we just stay off the path!"

When they arrived back at the beach, Ruth instructed the girls to run as fast as they could, jump into their submarines, and submerge beneath the water so as not to be discovered by Colossus.

"We all go on my count!" Ruth ordered. "Hold your breath in case they try to gas us again. Run as fast as you can, and don't stop until you're in your submarine and underwater!"

The girls nodded and braced themselves for a sandy sprint.

"One, two, three, GO!" shouted Ruth.

Anna decided she would be the last to arrive at her sub even though she was the fastest runner. She helped Natasha into her Aquadoodle and closed the hatch.

"Turn on your intercom," Anna said. "I'll check on you when we all get underwater!"

It was hard to believe, but the girls felt more secure in their Aquadoodles than they did back on land. They formed a circle about fifty feet offshore and waited for instructions.

"I still think we should go back to the ship!" Grace pleaded as she clicked on her intercom for everyone to hear.

"Grace? Come in, Grace, is that you?"

The voice was difficult to make out at first, but then as it repeated the question, it became clear. It was Isabela, Abby-Marie, and Lily.

"What happened to you guys? We were up all-night worrying!"

"We were captured!" said Evie. "We spent the whole night in a shipping container!"

"Yes, and they took our doodle dogs too!" said Mikako. "We have to rescue them! We don't have much time!"

"They must be swimming out to the middle of the bay by now!" said Abby-Marie. "Something is out there, and I know it's the reason behind all this madness. I say we change course and find out what it is!"

Back on the Seadoodle, Sven was frantically trying to open the door of the ship's bridge attempting to free the groggy professors piled on the floor. He found a crowbar from the machine room, but the metal was too thick to wedge into the doorway and pry it open. Then he realized he could get in another way. He swung the crowbar hard enough to crack the window and removed all the loose glass and climbed in.

"Change course…" Captain Carlos struggled to speak. "Change course! Manual mode!"

Sven looked out at the ocean and could see that the ship was leaving the bay and heading out to sea.

"We have to get to whatever it is in the middle of the bay!" he said to the group of professors drooling on the floor. "If we can shut off those radio frequencies, we can stop these people!"

Sven looked around at the hundreds of controls in front of him. He found the switch labeled manual mode and turned it on.

"Uh, uh, uh," said The Dentist from the screen in front of him. "Don't try to be a hero, Mr. Sven. If you go looking for my ship, I'm afraid you will have to pay the consequences. Dire consequences!"

Lily, Isabela, and Abby-Marie changed course, hoping to be the first to arrive in the middle of the bay.

"Ruth, it looks like we might get there a few minutes ahead of you," said Lily over the intercom. "We're going to take a look around and let you know what we find."

When the three girls arrived at the spot in the bay that was indicated by the GPS trackers, they came to a stop and brought their submarines to the surface.

"Nothing! There's nothing here!" said Isabela.

"This is hopeless!" said Abby-Marie. "We're never going to find them!"

Lily was beginning to think Abby-Marie was right when she spotted something in the sky.

"Isabela, Abby-Marie, look to the right! Do you see those heat vapors rising over the water? My guess is there's a ship over there using a cloaking device."

The three girls maneuvered their submarines toward the rising heat, not sure what they might find. As they approached the position, they broke through an invisible screen and bumped into a large ship.

"This is it!" shouted Lily. "This is the source of all our problems!"

"But how do we get on board?" asked Isabela.

"On board?" asked Abby-Marie. "I'm NOT going on board!"

"We have to!" said Lily. "You two need to climb on top of my submarine, and I'll lift you up so you can grab the railing and get on board."

"But I'm afraid of the water!" cried Abby-Marie. "I don't want to get out of my Aquadoodle!"

"You have to," said Isabela. "They're going to program our doodles, just like they did to that bird!"

Abby-Marie knew Isabela was right.

"Okay, I'll do it, but I want Edison and Galileo to come with us," said Abby-Marie.

"Fine," said Lily, "but you two need to get on that ship now! I'll lift your doodles onto the deck right after you get on board."

Abby-Marie pulled her submarine next to Lily's and climbed onto the top of her glass cockpit. Isabela joined her as the two grabbed the ship's railing and climbed on deck.

"Look!" whispered Isabela. The two girls peered through a large window and saw a long row of dentist chairs.

"It's the doodles! They have our Wonder Doodles!"

25

THE SS TOOTHACHE

"I can't look!" shouted Abby-Marie as she turned her face away from the window and slumped onto the deck.

Inside the white spotless room, seven drowsy Wonder Doodles were strapped to oversized dentist chairs. The procedure had already begun. Large mechanical arms at each station worked in perfect synchronization as they restrained, stretched, and glued. The dogs felt no pain, only the pressure of being worked on by the computer-controled robots. In seconds, a single glowing blue tooth was glued into their mouths. Instantaneously, their brains began receiving remote-controlled radio signals. They had no choice but to obey the orders from their new master thousands of miles away.

"Is it over?" asked Abby-Marie.

"The tooth part," answered Isabela, "But I can't quite figure it out what they're doing now. It looks like the robots are trying to strap something onto their backs!"

The large metal robots grabbed each of the puppies, flipped them over, and placed them on the floor. Two mechanical arms strapped a pack with a large magnetic disk on their backs. A red light on the side of the pack started blinking.

"It's a backpack of some sort, but I can't figure out what it's for," said Isabela. "Abby-Marie, would you PLEASE stand up and look? I need you to help me figure out what's going on here!"

Abby-Marie slowly stood up and looked again through the window. The seven dogs had flashing waterproof packs attached to their torsos. Their legs were shaking, and they were all a bit wobbly from the gas.

Abby-Marie gasped. "I'm no expert, but if I didn't know any better, I'd say those things were bombs!"

Isabela swallowed hard as she felt the lump in her throat start to grow. She knew Abby-Marie was right.

"What do we do?" she asked.

"We have to deactivate them!" said Abby-Marie. "There must be a computer control room on this ship. If we find it, we can hack into the system. It's the only way we can shut it down!"

Isabela and Abby-Marie ducked below the window and ran their hands along the wall of the ship. They stopped at each window trying to figure out which room contained the computer control center. When they reached the bow of the ship they stopped as an eerie glow poured from the window above them.

"This has to be it!" said Isabela, placing her hand against the door that led inside. She raised her hand and grabbed the door handle. "Are you sure you want to do this?"

"No," Abby-Marie said surprised by the question. "What I want is to go back to bed so I can wake up from this terrible nightmare!"

Isabela frowned. "Sorry I asked," she said apologetically. "I don't think we have a choice." She turned the knob and the door clicked open.

Once inside, the girls stood engulfed in the glow of computer screens and technology. The room was clean and bright just like the dentist room at the back of the ship. The girls started scanning the controls for clues. There had to be a way to deactivate the bombs!

"Looking for something?" said The Dentist as his masked face appeared before them on a large computer screen. "I believe it's Isabela and Abby-Marie if I'm not mistaken. Why, it's a pleasure to meet you," said The Dentist with dripping sarcasm. "I've already had the pleasure of meeting your schoolmates on the island. And….your professors, well I've had the pleasure of meeting them too. So, is that everyone?"

"Who are you, and what are you doing with our dogs?" demanded Isabela.

"Again, with the questions. You Wonderwood people are all alike. Questions, questions, questions! I told you, I'm The Dentist. I work for Colossus, and our goal is to rule the world. Your dogs are mere pawns in my plan. They will be my slaves for the rest of their lives!"

"You won't get away with this!" shouted Abby-Marie.

"Well, I must say, you Wonderwood Girls sure have been making it hard for me," The Dentist laughed. "That's why you've forced me to go from Project Tooth Implantation to Project Extinction!"

"Extinction?" the two girls gulped.

"That's right, Project Extinction! If you girls would have taken the hint and moved out of this bay, I wouldn't have to take such drastic measures, but you've given me no choice!"

"But you DO have a choice!" shouted Isabela at the screen. "You can let us all go!"

"What, and have you report me to the authorities? Oh, that will never do," laughed the man behind the computer screen. "I'm afraid the only option you've given me is to sink your ship. Then you'll all have to leave, won't you?"

"My mom and dad are on that ship!" screamed Isabela.

"They all should have left when they had the chance," said The Dentist calmly. "Now, take a look out the window. Do you see your Wonder Doodles all lined up to take a swim?"

The girls looked out the window and saw seven dogs lined up with flashing harnesses strapped to their backs.

"Those backpacks are magnetic bombs set to explode in fifteen minutes," said The Dentist. "I've timed it perfectly. Your furry little friends will swim under your ship and attach these bombs to the bottom of your precious Seadoodle. I love it when I can get animals to do my dirty work!"

"You're evil!" shouted Abby-Marie.

"No, I just don't like it when people get in my way," snarled The Dentist.

"Well, that's exactly what we plan to do," answered Isabela as she tried to turn off the control room by pulling plugs and flipping switches. Abby-Marie joined her as they frantically tried to shut the system down.

"Uh-uh-uh!" shouted The Dentist. "I said don't touch the buttons! Now it looks like I need to put you two to sleep as well!"

The Dentist flipped a switch, and the control room door flew open. A seagull swooped in and filled the room with laughing gas.

"Sleep tight!" laughed The Dentist.

The two girls fell to the floor, held their breath, and started crawling toward the door. The door was closing fast when a small furry paw shoved its way through. The two girls couldn't believe it. Galileo and Edison were dragging a scuba tank with their mouths. They pushed through the doorway and dropped the tank in front of the two girls. Isabela immediately took a deep breath from the tank and then handed the regulator to Abby-Marie. The two dogs were overcome by the gas and fell fast asleep.

"We have to jump overboard!" shouted Isabela, grabbing the tank in one hand and Abby-Marie around the waist with the other. Isabela pushed to the edge of the ship and the two girls tumbled over the railing. As the smoke cleared in the control room, red LED timers started ticking down.

15:00

14:59

14:58

14:57…

26
SINKING DOWN

The two girls were plummeting down to the water below, but somehow, they seemed to be falling in super slow motion. Isabela was falling with her back to the water, and Abby-Marie was falling forward, the two girls were staring at each other face to face with the metal scuba tank sandwiched between them. As they fell, Isabela looked up at Abby-Marie, and for the first time, she felt the same fear Abby-Marie had been feeling from the moment they arrived.

Abby-Marie also felt something new. Falling in slow motion seemed like an eternity, but it gave her time to consider the look on Isabela's face. For the first time she felt sympathy for her. All she wanted to do was share her island paradise with her classmates, and ever since they arrived in the Galápagos, Isabela's whole world had been falling apart. And yet, here she was, holding her around the waist as they fell together into the sea. It was a profound moment, but it was quickly shattered as the two girls slammed into the water below.

"Isabela, I, I, I can't move!" shouted Abby-Marie taking in a mouth full of saltwater. "Isabela, help me!" she pleaded as she felt herself starting to sink.

But Isabela didn't respond. The metal scuba tank smashed against her head when they struck the water, producing a large gash that was starting to bleed.

"No!" shouted Abby-Marie as she watched Isabela go unconscious. "You can't leave me! I need you!"

Abby-Marie could feel the grip of Isabela's hand release from around her waist and realized her friend was about to sink below the surface. She looked around for help and saw the seven Wonder Doodles diving into the water with flashing explosive packs strapped to their backs.

"Joey! Gutenburg!" she shouted. "Over here, guys! Please, come here! I need your help!"

But the dogs swam past her like machines. They had been

programmed to deliver the deadly package strapped to their backs and they had no other choice but to obey.

"Please," she whimpered as the dogs swam away. "Please…"

Isabela was still unconscious, and her body went limp as her head fell face forward into the water. Abby-Marie froze. She felt Isabela's hand slip away and then watched as her classmate's head disappeared below the surface.

"Theo!" she cried. She saw herself standing on the deck of that yacht when she was a little girl. She saw her brother. She felt that terrible moment when he fell overboard and nearly drowned. "Theo, no!"

Abby-Marie felt Isabela's hand slide down her leg, past her ankle, as her body sank out of sight.

"I can't move!" shouted Abby-Marie. "Mom, Dad, help! Isabela is drowning! I'm drowning! I can't…"

The shock of it all was overwhelming. Her legs and arms were paralyzed with fear. "Please, I don't want to die," she cried out desperately. Abby-Marie was locked in her own body—a body that refused to move, that refused to swim.

"It's no use," she whispered in defeat. Abby-Marie

dropped her head in the water and surrendered to the sea. She sank below the surface and followed her friend Isabela who was already halfway to the bottom of the ocean floor.

27

LILY GOES TO THE DENTIST

Lily's whole body was trembling. She was so worried she thought she might throw up all over the controls of her submarine.

"Abby-Marie and Isabela should've been back by now!" she thought.

She couldn't decide if she should go look for her two friends or continue waiting in the spot where she left them. She decided to wait. Lily frantically searched the water above her, she saw something break the surface with a splash. Cousteau started barking. It was Isabela's

Wonder Doodle, Galileo. There was a second smaller splash that followed as Abby-Marie's Maltipoo, Edison, jumped in behind him. A blueish light escaped from their mouths.

"He's got them too!" shouted Lily. "He's got Galileo and Edison!"

The dogs swam past the glass cockpit of Lily's submarine with a blank zombie-like expression on their faces. Both dogs had a blinking bomb strapped to their backs!

"Come in! Can anyone hear me?" Lily clicked on her intercom, hoping for help to arrive.

"Lily? Come in, Lily! Where are you?" Ruth responded when she heard Lily's voice come over the intercom. "Lily, we're on our way! We're only a few minutes from your location!"

"You need to hurry!" shouted Lily. "It's Colossus! They've captured Abby-Marie and Isabela and they're being held hostage on a ship by an evil man called The Dentist. I sent Galileo and Edison to rescue them, but now he has them too!"

"We're on our way!" said Ruth. "You stay put, and when we get there, we'll get them back!"

"I don't know if that's the best plan," said Lily. "They've got bombs!"

"Bombs?!?" gasped Ruth.

"The Wonder Doodles," said Lily. "He's strapped bombs to their backs, and they're swimming to the Seadoodle now. It looks like he's going to blow up our ship!"

"What should we do?" asked Ruth.

"I think you guys should go after the doodles!" answered Lily. "If we don't deactivate those bombs, we stand to lose our ship, our puppies, and our professors!"

"Got it!" Ruth responded. "Okay Wonderwood Girls," she shouted over the intercom. "Change of plans! We need to locate our doodles and make sure those bombs on their backs don't explode!"

Lily clicked off her intercom and looked back at Cousteau.

"What should we do, boy?" she asked.

Cousteau looked into Lily's eyes. Somehow, he knew what she was asking and answered. "Woof!"

"I agree," answered Lily. "We're going in. It's time to get

our friends back!"

Lily put her Aquadoodle in reverse and turned the mini submarine toward the back of the ship in front of her. She positioned the sub in the center of the large black conveyor belt and nudged forward. The nose of the submarine caught the belt and it started to pull them onto the ship.

"No turning back now," said Lily to her furry friend seated behind her.

The conveyor belt pulled the small craft into the large white room lined with dentist chairs. Lily pulled a lever and released the air pressure from her submarine. The glass hatch opened, and she stepped out onto the floor with Cousteau limping behind her.

"What is this place?" she gasped.

"It's my office!" answered The Dentist from the computer monitor mounted on the wall. "What are you doing on my ship, Lily Fernbush?"

"How do you know my name?" asked Lily, with a growing sense of fear.

"I know everything about you, Lily," answered The Dentist. "Your name is Lily Fernbush. You're eight years old. You were born and raised in London, England. You have a photographic memory, and I believe it is for that reason you have been selected to be a student at the famous Wonderwood Academy."

"Where are my friends?" Lily demanded.

"How should I know?" said The Dentist. "I think they jumped overboard."

"What did you do to Galileo and Edison?" shouted Lily.

"I did a little dental work," said The Dentist. "So now, I have control over nine of the ten Wonder Doodles, and it appears I will soon have control over number ten!"

A robotic arm reached down and grabbed Cousteau by the back and planted him firmly in one of the dentist chairs. Cousteau howled in pain.

"You're hurting him!" Lily screamed.

"Oh, that's right," said The Dentist. "Forgive me, we've somehow forgotten a very important step: the laughing gas!" The man behind the screen turned a switch, and gas began to fill the room. Lily realized what was happening and dashed for the scuba tank in her submarine. She pulled the regulator to her mouth, opened the air valve, and took a deep breath.

"Stop!" she shouted through the mouthpiece.

"What was that?" asked The Dentist laughing. "It sounded like you said 'schwop'. What does that mean? Schwop?"

Lily took another deep breath and pulled the regulator from her mouth. "Let him go!" she shouted. "He has a broken leg. He's no good to you!"

"You underestimate your furry little friend," answered The Dentist. "Besides, we all know he's going to heal in a few weeks, and by then I'll have plenty of seaweed for him to harvest."

Lily put the regulator back in her mouth and grabbed the robotic arm that was preparing to glue a glowing blue tooth into Cousteau's mouth. Lily was dangling from the metal arm with one hand and trying hard not to drop the scuba tank she was holding in her other hand.

"Oh my, you are a brave little girl!" said The Dentist. "You're the kind of person we're looking for here at Colossus. Any chance you might be interested in joining my work force too?"

The Dentist clicked another button, and a robotic arm from the next dentist chair grabbed the scuba tank from

Lily's hand. A second arm wrapped around her waist and jammed her in the chair next to Cousteau. The gas in the room quickly took its effect.

"Well, I didn't see that coming," said The Dentist to himself. "I thought we were going to only work on animals, but this is really the next logical next step. One eight-year-old girl from England under my control. How convenient. Finally, a remote-control worker who can talk!"

28

THE BLACK WOLF

Back in the water, Abby-Marie was sinking fast. The weight of the scuba tank was pulling her to the bottom at twice the speed of Isabela who was ten feet below her, still bleeding and unconscious. It wasn't long before Abby-Marie passed out and fell unconscious too.

As everything went black, she saw an image of herself standing in a deep dark cave. She was cold, soaking wet, and unable to move. She saw warm sunlight outside of the cave, but she couldn't move. Her family was outside playing in the sun, and they were calling to her.

"Abby-Marie, come be with us! Why are you still in that

dark, ugly cave? Come outside. It's warm and sunny!"

Abby-Marie couldn't understand why she couldn't just walk outside to be with her family, but then the reason became clear. She saw a strange moving shadow. It was just an outline at first, but then it came into focus as the object moved to block her way out. When the shadow was directly in front of her, she could see that it was a fierce, black wolf that was bigger than any wild animal she had ever seen. Its fur was caked with dirt and mud, and it growled at her, revealing two rows of sharp, glowing blue teeth.

"I can't come!" The words formed in her mind, but nothing came out. "Mom, I can't. There's a big wolf, and he's going to eat me!"

She heard her mom's voice again. "Oh, please come, Abby-Marie! I've made some macarons. They're your favorite!"

Her dad and her brother were calling her too. They seemed to be playing a game, but she couldn't tell what game it was. She only knew they were having fun, and she couldn't move.

She tried to say, "I can't!" but instead she started to cry.

"Why are you letting that wolf stand in your way?" her

brother shouted from outside the cave. "He's keeping you from so many wonderful things!"

"Yes, so many wonderful things!" chimed a chorus of friends.

Abby-Marie looked again and saw all her classmates at the Wonderwood Academy. Lily was playing with Cousteau, and Anna was flying around on her Wonder Disc.

"Don't bother trying with her!" interrupted Isabela as she stuck out a finger and pointed at Abby-Marie. "She's a hopeless case!"

"Hopeless?" thought Abby-Marie. "Who is she to say I'm a hopeless case?"

Abby-Marie felt her sadness turn to anger, and then felt her anger to rage. She looked up again and saw Lady Burd walk toward the entrance of the cave.

"Oh, I see you still have poison in your pocket," said Lady Burd. "Why don't you give all that poison to the wolf?"

Abby-Marie looked down and saw that her two pockets were jammed full of Sven's tiny little sausages. There were so many sausages in her pockets that they were falling on the ground all around her. The angry wolf growled again. It lunged forward and grabbed her hand with its long, sharp teeth.

"Hey! Leave me alone!"

Abby-Marie suddenly discovered she was no longer frozen. For the first time, she could move. She wrestled her bleeding hand from the wolf's mouth and quickly started to empty her pockets.

"Here! These are for you!" she shouted at the black wolf as he started to devour the tiny sausages. "I'm tired to keeping these awful things in my pockets!" She threw the sausages in the air, and watched the wild animal gobble them up as fast as he could, and then she saw what she needed to see. She saw the big black wolf fall.

And as the wolf hit the ground, Abby-Marie's motionless body struck the sandy bottom of the ocean floor. The impact caused the regulator in her hand to engage, and large bubbles filled the water around her. Air bubbles were escaping with a huge force, and they began filling her nose and mouth. Her head was thrown back as the force of the air gave her no choice but to breathe. She opened her eyes and was quickly reminded of the desperate situation she was in, but this time instead of being frozen with fear, she was filled with a will to fight.

"I'm not missing out on those macrons! I'm not missing out on anything!" she said to herself as she stuffed the regulator back in her mouth. "And, Isabela, neither are you!"

Abby-Marie looked over and saw Isabela just a few feet away. She took a deep breath of air from the tank, pulled the regulator from her mouth, and slipped it in front of Isabela's face. She released some air into her nose, and then worked the regulator in her mouth trying to fill her lungs with fresh air.

"Come on, Isabela!" she shouted in the water. "Let's get out of this dark cave!"

Abby-Marie had been a strong swimmer before Theo's accident, and it was only that awful memory that kept her from the water. Once the fear was gone, it all came back to her. She wrapped her arm around Isabela's body and started swimming back to the surface.

"Hang in there Isabela! Just a few more feet!"

Once the two girls broke the surface, Abby-Marie pulled Isabela's head back and started giving her mouth-to-mouth.

"Come on, Isabela, breathe!" she shouted as she continued to fill Isabela's lungs with air. "We have bombs to deactivate!"

Isabela didn't move. She had been underwater for quite some time, and the gash on her forehead was swollen and bleeding.

"You can't die!" shouted Abby-Marie, and in desperation she slapped Isabela in the face.

Isabela's eyes flew open as she vomited the gallon of seawater that was in her stomach. She looked up and slapped Abby-Marie right back.

"What was that for?" Isabela shouted at Abby-Marie. "Can't you see I'm wounded?"

"Isn't that what you're supposed to do when you have somebody's back?" said Abby-Marie happy to see her friend alive.

"I guess you think this makes us even," said Isabela in a huff.

"No," answered Abby-Marie, "I think this means we're friends!"

29
THE COUNTDOWN

"What do you want me to do, Mr. Dentist?" asked Lily, staring blankly at her new master on the computer screen in front of her.

"I want you to destroy the Wonderwood Academy!" answered The Dentist. "You have ten minutes to blow up your ship and make sure all your professors and classmates leave these islands forever!"

Lily snapped to attention like a soldier and saluted the screen. "Yes sir!" she responded, as the blue tooth in her mouth glowed even brighter.

Back in the water, Abby-Marie was struggling to figure out what they needed to do next. "We have to figure out how to deactivate those bombs!" she said desperately. She was holding onto Isabela and struggling to keep the two of them afloat.

"I can't!" cried Isabela. "I'm hurt. I can barely move!"

"We have to try!" said Abby-Marie. "Let's get to our submarines and ask the other girls for help!"

Abby-Marie let go of the scuba tank in her hand and let it sink to the bottom. She wrapped her arm around Isabela's waist and started swimming. She kicked with her feet, struggling to pull them both through the water and back to safety.

"Isabela, you have to help me!" she pleaded. "I can't get you back into your sub without your help!"

Isabela reached up with both hands, and with the little strength she had left, she helped pull herself back into the cockpit of her Aquadoodle as Abby-Marie pushed from behind.

Lily climbed back into her submarine as The Dentist reversed the conveyor belt and returned her to the water below.

"Calling all Wonderwood Girls!" Lily called over the intercom. "Attention all Wonderwood Girls, please go back to the island. We've got things under control. I repeat," ordered Lily, "return to the island now!"

"That makes no sense!" responded Ruth. "Lily, what are you talking about? Guys, don't listen to Lily! I think Colossus has control of her too! Everyone stay on course!"

Once Isabela and Abby-Marie were back in their submarines, Abby-Marie switched on the intercom.

"Wonderwood Girls, where are you?" called Abby-Marie, trying to contact her classmates. "This dentist guy is crazy. He's got bombs strapped to the backs of our Wonder Doodles and he's going to blow up the Seadoodle! We must warn Dr. Tusen-Takk and the professors. We have to deactivate those bombs!"

"No," interrupted Lily. "Abby-Marie is just having

another one of her moments! Everything here is under control. It would be safer if you all went back to the island!"

"That's a lie!" shouted Abby-Marie. "What's going on with you, Lily? Guys don't listen to Lily! We need you to cut those bomb packs off the Wonder Doodles, and you must do it now. We only have a few minutes before they all explode!"

"I say we listen to Abby-Marie!" said Anna Andersen. "Let's save our doodle dogs now!"

30
BOMBS AWAY

Sven didn't know what to do next. He looked down and saw Dr. Tusen-Takk and a pile of sleeping professors on the floor.

"I sure could use some help!" he said. "Please, professors, wake up!"

Anna's doodle dog, Galileo, was just a few yards away from placing the first magnetic bomb on the Seadoodle's metal hull. Ruth was the first to arrive; she quickly used the harvesting tools on the front of her submarine to cut the straps off Galileo's backpack, and the bomb sank to the bottom of the bay.

She surfaced her submarine and opened her cockpit, trying to get the attention of her professors on the ship's deck. "Help!" she yelled as loudly as she could.

Sven heard her screaming and ran outside.

"What's happening?" Sven shouted in confusion.

"Bombs! They've got bombs!" answered Ruth. "Some crazy guy who calls himself The Dentist is trying to blow up our ship! You guys need to get out of there fast!"

"The professors have all been gassed," answered Sven. "They can't swim!"

"Put a life jacket on them and throw them overboard!" shouted Ruth. "You have to get them off the ship before it explodes!"

The other girls were frantic. They were driving their submarines just below the surface, trying desperately to find the other dogs. Natasha located her dog, DaVinci, and positioned her submarine underneath him and quickly cut the straps of the bomb pack and watched it fall to the ocean floor.

"How many bombs are left?" shouted Mikako, scanning

the water around her.

"We have to keep count!" answered Ruth. "We need to make sure we get all of them!"

"And we need to do it before we run out of time!" shouted Evie. "How much time is left before these things explode?"

"Four minutes!" answered Lily from the cockpit of her submarine. "Do you want me to count down the seconds for you?"

"What's wrong with you, Lily?" screamed Abby-Marie. "It's like you're working for Colossus!"

"I am!" answered Lily with a laugh. "Three minutes and fifty seconds, girls!"

31

CHAOS IN THE BAY

"They're going to sink our ship!" shouted Grace.

"Not if we sink their ship first!" said Abby-Marie. "Isabela, do you remember how you pushed my submarine at the seaweed farm?"

Isabela was barely conscious. "Sure," she whispered. "Why are you bringing that up now? I thought we were friends."

"We are!" shouted Abby-Marie as she turned her submarine around and positioned her propeller against the hull of the Colossus ship. "Remember how we're supposed to say to each other, 'I've got your back'? Well, right now, I need you to have my FRONT! I need you to push my submarine into the hull of that ship!"

Isabela struggled to sit up. She could see what Abby-Marie was trying to do. The two small submarines were now facing nose to nose. "Isabela, when I give you the signal, I want you to start pushing my submarine as hard as you can!" shouted Abby-Marie, "We're sending this floating dentist office to the bottom of the sea!"

Back in the water, the other girls were frantically trying to locate their dogs and cutting the bombs from their backs.

"That's six!" shouted Ruth. "Only three more to go!"

"No, you have four more to go!" Lily corrected. "Cousteau will be there shortly. He's working for us now too. And by the way, you now have two minutes and ten seconds!"

On the deck of the Seadoodle, Sven was busy dragging bodies to the ship's railing. He grabbed Dr. Tusen-Takk's arms and shoved her into a life vest as he lifted her body and threw her overboard. "Lady Burd, you're next!" he

248

said to the oldest member of the faculty. "I'll try to make this as painless as possible," and he dropped her into the sea.

"Eight!" shouted Ruth. "We have eight bombs at the bottom! We need to find the other two!"

"One minute!" shouted Lily over the intercom. "This is really getting exciting," she laughed again. "I do hope to see some fireworks soon!"

The professors continued to splash into the water as Ruth tried to corral the floating faculty into a group. "We have less than a minute, Sven!" she shouted above her. "You need to get everyone off the ship, and then you need to get yourself off too!"

Abby-Marie and Isabela put their submarines into overdrive, Isabela pushing forward and Abby-Marie in reverse. The blades of Abby-Marie's propellor started taking chunks out of The Dentist's ship.

"Keep pushing!" shouted Abby-Marie. "Dr. Yaron told us these propellors could cut through the hull of a ship, and right now, we need them to do just that!"

The sound of metal tearing into the fiberglass hull was

terrifying. Large pieces of the ship's hull were thrown in every direction as the evil ship started to fill with water.

"You're too late!" shouted Lily. "Your ship is going to explode!"

"Not if yours sinks first!" shouted Abby-Marie.

"Nine!" shouted Ruth, as she watched Mikako cut the bomb pack from her little puppy, Newton. "That leaves one to go! Quick, girls, find that bomb!"

Ruth looked up and saw her father falling into the water next to her.

"Look out below!" shouted Sven. He was standing on the railing of the ship with his sausage grinder in his arms. He took a deep breath and jumped.

"Thirty seconds!" shouted Lily.

Cousteau was the last dog to enter the water with a bomb on its back.

"Last one!" shouted Ruth. "C'mon, Anna, let's see how fast these little submarines can go!"

The two girls pushed their steering wheels forward, racing as fast as they could toward Cousteau, who was struggling to swim with a broken leg.

The two girls reached the wet and wounded Dalmadoodle in just a few seconds. Ruth lifted his body out of the water, and Anna rushed in and cut the straps, causing the bomb to sink to the bottom of the sea.

"Hah!" shouted Ruth. "All ten bombs are at the bottom, and we still have twenty seconds to go!"

"Oh, that's what you think," countered Lily, who strategically placed her submarine just below them and caught the last bomb with her mechanical arms. "I still have twenty seconds to make sure this bomb does exactly what it was made for!"

Lily pushed her steering wheel forward and rushed toward the Seadoodle. Ruth and Anna tried to catch her, but Lily was too far ahead of them. Lily started to count down over the intercom.

"Ten, nine, eight, seven, six…"

Lily attached the magnetic bomb to the hull of the ship and darted for cover.

"…five, four, three, two, one!"

KAAABOOM!

The explosion blew a hole the size of a small school bus in the side of the Seadoodle. The explosion was so powerful that it threw Lily, Ruth, and Anna out of their submarines and into the water.

Fifty feet below the surface of the water, the other nine bombs detonated with a tremendous blast. The force of the explosions looked like volcanos erupting in the middle of the bay.

The Seadoodle started sinking. The Dentist's ship was sinking too, and when its control bridge went underwater, the radio transmissions ceased. The air went silent, and thousands of birds, turtles, sea lions, and other creatures came back to life!

"My mouth hurts!" said Lily as she pressed her fingers against the blue tooth in her jaw. "What happened? Why am I floating in the water, and why is everyone staring at me?"

Everyone watched as the two ships on either side of them sank to the bottom of the sea.

32

ALL WASHED UP

It took over an hour to get everyone out of the water and onto the beach. The Wonderwood Girls were exhausted, but somehow, they managed to pull their groggy professors out of the water and into the back of their submarines. Ruth pulled out her camera and started filming the rescue.

"Where am I?" asked Dr. Tusen-Takk, dazed and confused.

"Lily blew up our ship," said Ruth. "We've taken you to shore."

"Oh, that's nice," answered Dr. Tusen-Takk with slurred speech. "I didn't really like that ship anyway."

All the professors were struggling to speak. The events of the day were still a blur as the effects of the laughing gas slowly started to wear off. Sven gathered sticks and branches and built a fire.

"Did someone throw me off the ship?" asked Lady Burd.

"Ya," Sven answered. "I threw you all off the ship and into the sea."

"What happened to my ship?" asked Captain Carlos.

"Lily blew it up!" said Anna.

"That's not good," said the captain, trying to warm himself by the fire.

"No, Dad, it's not," said Isabela, putting her arms around her mom and dad, "but we're alive!"

"And we got rid of that awful dentist ship that Colossus was using to turn all the animals into slaves!" said Abby-Marie. "Look, the animals are free again!"

Abby-Marie pointed to the path leading into the jungle.

Hundreds of animals were walking back to the water. They no longer looked like zombies but wild animals that seemed very happy to be free.

"Hector has a lot of work ahead of him," said Grace. "He's going to need a small army to pull all those blue teeth and remove all those baskets!"

"Hector?" said Dr. Tusen-Takk coming back to her old self. "Oh, no! Hector is coming! He's going to inspect the kennels. We're not ready! We're going to get expelled!

"Oh, I think we're way past the inspection," said Anna. "I think we need to start looking for a new school."

As the weight of Anna's words started to sink in, three military helicopters flew in over the palm trees and hovered overhead. Ropes were lowered, and soldiers with helmets and guns rappelled to the beach below. Hector the Inspector had already assembled a small army, and the second his boots hit the sand he took control.

"What were those explosions?" he shouted. "Why are these dogs on the beach? Put out that fire!"

"¡*Cálmate, hermano*!" said Nina looking up at her brother. "You should be thanking these girls! They solved the mystery of all those missing animals and destroyed the invisible Colossus ship. The Galápagos are safe again!"

"But the kennels!" protested Hector.

"Oh, tío, please stop!" cried Isabela as she stood to hug her uncle. "I almost died. We all almost died. If it wasn't for my friend Abby-Marie, I would have drowned at the bottom of that bay."

Hector softened. "Wow, I'm glad you're all alive," he answered, "but I still want you off this island. The Wonderwood Academy has to find somewhere else to have school."

"Can I get my tooth fixed first?" asked Lily pulling down her lip and revealing a large blue tooth.

"Well, that's two schools destroyed in less than a week," said Dr. Tusen-Takk, holding her hands to the hockey helmet that protected her head. "I think we need to find someplace quiet. Someplace in the countryside with no one around for miles. It needs to be a peaceful place, like a convent or monastery."

"As long as were all together!" said Isabela, reaching out to hold Abby-Marie's hand.

"Do you think you'll need a chef?" asked Sven, pulling his sausage grinder to his chest with a grin.

"Did you say monastery?" asked Abby-Marie. "I think I might just have the perfect place."

"Go on…" said Dr. Tusen-Takk said as everyone leaned in.

Abby-Marie smiled the biggest smile of her life. "How would you guys like spend the rest of the semester in France?"

WONDERWOOD GIRLS CLASSIFIED ★

For more
information on the series:

wonderwoodgirls.com

Made in the USA
Monee, IL
27 February 2024

53700876R00150